READING THE COUNTRY

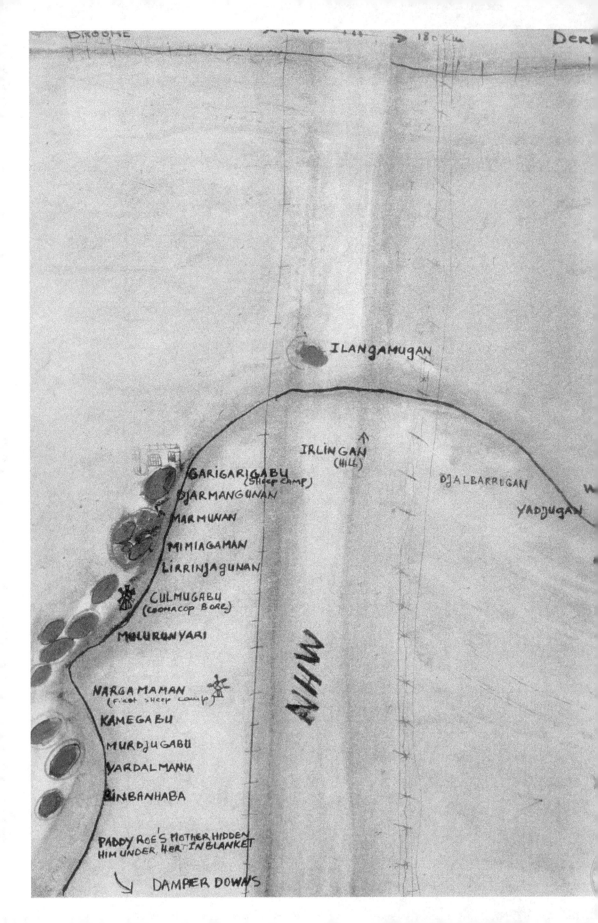

NADABURUNLGRU
NARINAN
MENYUDAN
LARDAN
NULUBARN
ULLUL
IRGILIMANDJAMORI
KALEAENUN
WANGUMELEGUN
KILIBAGULAN
ANARWALIGNIAN
EDAR
Lake EDA

BARGARIGUN
KALBANGAGAN
NATINMARRA
BARKRAGAN
RARRDJALI
WANANAMBALBANA
RLUMBARLUMBARNGANANG
NGURULALA
YARRINGULU
WILIWA
LIRDARRINJUGAN
MARRIYANGARDA
BIYARRUGAN (Jerricop)
W. DAMP
(come-u
the Hill
WARRIANMAMAN
INJDJIDANA
DJULIRIRI
(Bervis Bore)

YELAYBIN
(like Dam, Turkey Nest)

BAL

MANIN WANDANAN
RANGGUNJARI
MARNINJGABU
(over flow Bore)

Spring
windmill

Bertram
'89

TRANSMISSION

Transmission denotes the transfer of information, objects or forces from one place to another, from one person to another. Transmission implies urgency, even emergency: a line humming, an alarm sounding, a messenger bearing news. Through Transmission interventions are supported, and opinions overturned. Transmission republishes classic works in philosophy, as it publishes works that re-examine classical philosophical thought. Transmission is the name for what takes place.

At the beginning of a journey, when you are about to cover strange territory, you are always ignorant and you have to rely on the local guides. They are the ones who know the safe tracks as well as places of danger ... one ignores the local guide at one's peril, for he is telling us how to survive in this country, and survival depends not just on the right sort of physical treatment of the country, but also on what one says about it, writes about it, and the images one makes of it.

Reading the Country is a journey into Roebuck Plains, near Broome in Australia's far north-west; it is an exploration of the meaning of place, an attempt to chart the relationships between people and those specific places in which they must find a place to live. It is a journey through landscape into language and ideas, and personal and cultural location.

> *... there are many things going on in the map of this book, depending where our gaze falls, or is drawn. A poetry, a politics of place, a theory, the perspectives, modes and languages of a painter, an Aboriginal man of high degree, a linguistic and anthropological theorist; paintings, recorded and transcribed narratives, photographs, geography ... this text has the quiet intelligence and turbulent tension of a poem.*
>
> Philip Mead, *Age Monthly Review*

> *A new dawn of literature ... As an event,* Reading the Country *is radical, innovative, unparalleled. No book like it has been produced in Australia.*
>
> Don Anderson, *National Times.*

> *... a splendid work and the collaboration involved in its generation is inspiring for its integrity, optimism and humility.*
>
> Dianne Johnson, *Sydney Morning Herald.*

> *... a powerful account of the Aboriginal sense of place. Highly recommended.*
>
> Robert Pascoe, *Australian Book review*

> *... an absorbing, beautifully produced book one that is deeply imbued with a sense of place ...*
>
> Laurie Clancy, *Sun-Herald.*

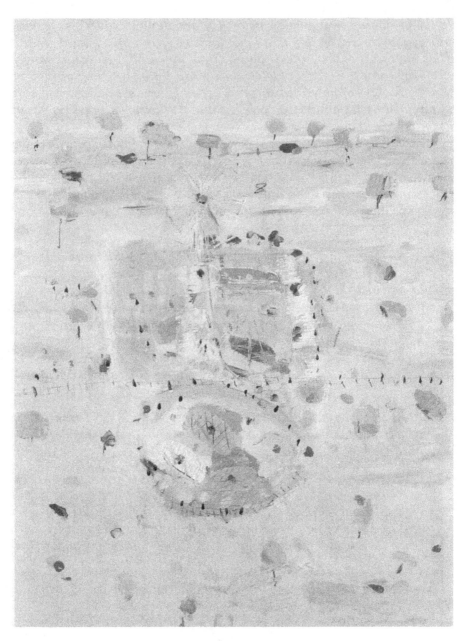

Nargananan—first sheep camp
1983, 76.5 cm x 57 cm, gouache and pastel on D'Arches paper

READING THE COUNTRY

INTRODUCTION TO NOMADOLOGY

Krim Benterrak
Stephen Muecke
Paddy Roe

With
Ray Keogh
Butcher Joe (Nangan)
E M Lohe

re.press

2014

re.press

PO Box 40, Prahran, 3181, Melbourne, Australia
http://www.re-press.org

This edition 2014

First published 1984 (Revised edition 1996) by
FREMANTLE ARTS CENTRE PRESS

Editor B R Coffey.

National Library of Australia Cataloguing-in-publication data

Benterrak, Krim, 1952- .
Reading The Country.

ISBN 978-0-9923734-2-9

1. Geographical perception. [2]. Aborigines, Australian — Western
Australia —
Roebuck Plains 3 Nomads — Western Australia — Roebuck Plains 4
Roebuck
Plains (W.A.) — Maps, Mental. I. Muecke, Stephen, 1951- .

Cover painting:
Roebuck Plains, 1984, 70.5 x 100cm, gouache and pastel on D'Arches
paper.

Page ii painting/map:
Reading The Country, 1984, 49 x 75.5cm, gouache, pastel and ink on
D'Arches paper.

To the
nomads of Broome,
always there and
always on the move

ACKNOWLEDGEMENTS TO FIRST EDITION

Many people contributed to the production of this book. While Eric Lohe, Butcher Joe (Nangan) and Ray Keogh made visible contributions, the ongoing criticism and support of Anna Haebich and Pru Black was invaluable to us. The continuing editorial task carried out by Ray Coffey of Fremantle Arts Centre Press, from the point when we first had the idea to the final production, confirmed for us the idea that authorship is not a private matter; so did the network of friends and readers: John Frow, Darrell Henry, Ian Hunter, Noel King, Humphrey McQueen, Douglas Muecke, Gary Wickham, Tim Willing and Peter Yu.

In Broome, David and Helen Morrell once again helped us by providing a place to work—and were wonderful friends. We are indebted to Glen McDonald of Roebuck Plains Station for his kindness in granting us access to the country.

We would like to thank the South Australian College of Advanced Education for covering the expenses of Paddy Roe and for granting Stephen Muecke ten weeks study leave from February to April 1982.

Krim Benterrak's paintings are reproduced courtesy of The Holmes a Court Collection. Special thanks to Belinda Carrigan and Anita Danby. Also to Kate McGurk for her assistance with photographing the paintings.

Acknowledgement must also be made to photographer Victor France for the reproduction of all of the paintings, and to the staff of the J S Battye Library of West Australian History and the Western Australian Department of Lands and Surveys for assistance in the research of parts of the book. The photograph on page 121 is reproduced by courtesy of the Western Australian Museum (from Lofgren, M E, *Patterns of Life*, Western Australian Museum Information Series: 6, Perth, 1975), the map on page 146 is reproduced by courtesy of the Western Australian Department of Lands and Surveys, and the document on page 147 is reproduced by courtesy of both the Department of Lands and Surveys and the J S Battye Library of West Australian History. The photograph on page 230 is courtesy of Peter Yu.

The maps on pages 18, 33, 34 and 65 and the illustrations on pages 105, 107 and 108 were drawn by Susan-Eve Barrow Ellvey.

Contents

Note to 1996 Edition

It is over a decade since this book was first published. In some ways the issues we raised then remain just as important. The 1992 Mabo decision represents a radical change in how the country is perceived in Australia; *terra nullius* is no longer a valid concept. Peter Yu, featured in this book, has continued the battle for indigenous rights in the Kimberley. He is now Chair of the Kimberley Land Council and was one of the architects of the Mabo decision. In the current struggle, it is not a question of merely laying claim to traditional lands, it is more a question of managing change, and managing and controlling a whole range of resources which affect Aboriginal people's lives.

Issues of Aboriginal history, oral and written, continue to be sources of great interest for both researchers and readers. In the Kimberley there is some urgency for this enormous amount of information to be collected as the custodians are getting older. Even in 1984 we were aware that we were only just touching a vast store of knowledge. Australians are coming to realise that Aboriginal knowledges and ways of living are a core part of national identity. As imperial histories fade away, post-colonial indigenous histories will come to occupy a dignified place in republican Australia.

The environmental imperatives are just as crucial as they always were, they are linked with 'resource management', they provide the checks and balances where economic greed threatens to get out of hand. But also, Aboriginal knowledge about the land is only just starting to be sensibly used. It sometimes clashes with notions of 'wilderness', with legitimated dispossession in the form of national parks, and with the romanticism which still wants to keep the 'native' in nature, as object of the tourist dollar.

These issues continue to be of concern to us as the original creators of *Reading the Country*, and we would tackle them again if we were to make a new book. For the new edition, however, we have left the original texts stand in their historical integrity.

Finally, we would like to express our sadness at the loss of Butcher Joe and Ray Keogh, companions who helped make it possible.

That's the hill I born

1983, 57 cm x 76.5 cm, gouache and pastel on D'Arches paper

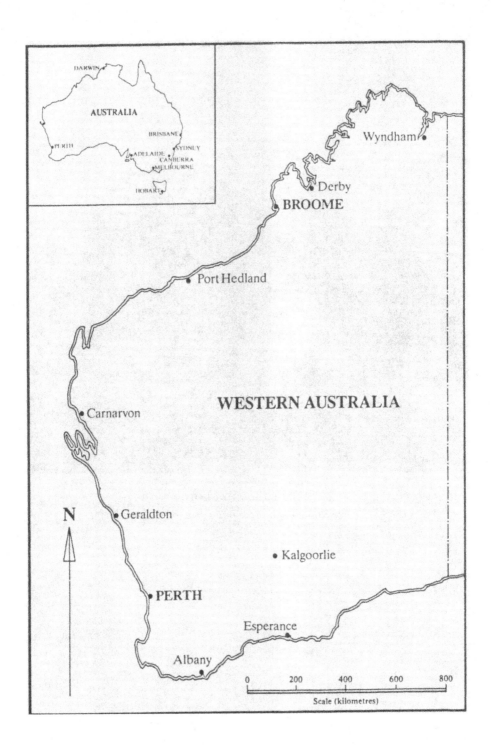

READING THIS BOOK

I venture to suggest that our age threatens one day to appear in the history of human culture as marked by the most dramatic and difficult trial of all, the discovery of and training in the meaning of the 'simplest' acts of existence: seeing, listening, speaking, reading—the acts which relate people to their works.

Althusser.

About one hundred years ago a place in North-West Australia, Roebuck Plains, was inhabited by Aboriginal people, the Yawur[1] (see map page 59). Today, the Yawur have merged into the Asian/Australian population of the nearby town of Broome, and the person who now knows the most about Roebuck Plains is a Nyigina man, Paddy Roe, who was born there at the time the first white people came to the country with their sheep. Only white people live permanently on Roebuck Plains now, and they run a Brahman cattle stud.

The Plains have been silent for quite a while; only the sounds of birds, lowing cattle, the chink of metal and orders shouted as fences and windmills are built. This book breaks that silence for a moment: voices speak, words are written and images are formed. It was Paddy Roe initially who had this desire to speak, to tell the story of his country once again. It was he who recognised in Krim Benterrak and myself our respective desires to paint and write. In the end, there is always this desire to create: to break through silence into form.

But with three authors one cannot imagine that the book is guided by any poetic unity or harmony. On the contrary, the poetry is of a different sort, one that responds to our times. It is a poetry of fragmentation, contradiction, unanswered questions, specificity, fluidity and change. We are three different people from three different cultures thrown together in a so-called multicultural society; or rather we are drawn together (with our different ways of expressing ourselves) by a concern

19

for one thing which remains constant in spite of everything: Roebuck Plains. Our speaking, writing and painting is in response, therefore, to what might be called a 'politics of place'.

In a more general sense this is an attempt to construct a theory of place, to find a method of charting the meanings of those specific places in which people must find a way to live in one manner or another: suburbs, office blocks, factories and farms. It just so happens that the place we are looking at is a little plain in North-West Australia.

This piece of country might be insignificant and it might also be 'full' of meanings. But how do we find out what it means, what its significance might be? What has drawn us towards making the idea of place central to our discourse? The answers to these questions will make our method clearer and at the same time distinguish it from other procedures which lead to different kinds of knowledge.

Roebuck Plains does not have an inherent meaning, nor is it heavily sign-posted so that visitors can be quite clear where they are and which way they should go to fulfil their purposes. Rather, the meanings of the Plains are constructed in language, that is, in dialogues which have a certain purpose or direction based on the sorts of signs, appropriate to their knowledge, which different people see in the country. So, generally, the botanist reads the country in terms of its plant life, the tourist in terms of its beauty, and so on.

Reading is not a perfectly natural activity which once mastered becomes automatic. A friend, Ian Hunter, once said that reading was somewhere between *breathing* and *judging. Breathing* is an automatic and natural activity most of the time, and *judging*, as in courts or beauty contests, is a highly social activity; it is so charged with social or cultural meaning that there is nothing natural about it. In spite of the years of training taken to achieve fluency in the skill of reading, it is largely taken for granted as an activity which enables one to see the meanings behind words straightaway.

The first factor limiting the contents of the book (and guiding its method) is the fact that the readings of any place are not infinite. They are perhaps theoretically infinite, but in practice, through history, certain readings appear, proliferate, then fade away when history no longer provides for them. An early reading of Roebuck Plains by a European (Dampier) tried to find possibilities of agriculture in it and things which would provide a basis for settlement. A very recent one, on the other hand, dates from the sixties and seventies and is made possible through the co-existence of the, perhaps transient, phenomena; hippies and cow dung. The itinerant hippy population of Broome sees in Roebuck Plains the possibility of collecting 'magic mushrooms'.

Nor are the possibilities of reading as numerous as the individuals who might come to this place. Although everyone might have their own private, mental response to a place, the reading only emerges as they attempt to 'express' this feeling: they must talk, sing, write, paint, take photographs and so on. These ways of representing things carry with them determined sets of meanings with which people can grapple, but with which they must of necessity start in their endeavour to make sense of things. Evidence for this lies in the widely differing Aboriginal and European responses to the country. Not even the wildest European imagination could produce Paddy Roe's reading of the country: the words are just not there. It makes more sense, therefore, to see the readings in terms of their cultural and historical determinations, rather than in terms of individual differences. To do the latter would also be to celebrate and reproduce the ideology of individualism which has such a high currency in Western societies.[2]

Why then, is *place* central to the theory and method of the book? Firstly, place introduces specificity and difference—new areas to be investigated within a larger whole. In Australia, the most commonly uttered place names refer to large unities: 'Australia', 'Melbourne', 'The Northern Territory' and even 'The Kimberleys'. These unities are so large they become abstract and general, they evoke stereotyped and familiar responses which feed off ideologies like nationalism, 'stateism' or the urban/rural division. The study of specific, local places puts things more on the scale of everyday living. This is not to say that the ideologies disappear at this level, but rather to suggest that one Scan see them working in what people say and do, in the tactics they employ.

Place, as a category, also displaces other dominant meanings which have been elevated by social ideologies to privileged positions. Categories like the Individual, the Family, Order, Democracy, Freedom and Authority are the taken-for-granted base terms around which other meanings cluster as if they lie at the origin of everything else. But these words are only signs which have emerged in the landscape of Western philosophy. Before them there were other signs going right back to the European oral traditions which we have lost, or take little notice of because they have been dominated by the written word.

Another reason for the emergence of place is the proliferation of ecological studies and the concept of world heritage; a new sensitivity is being demanded of people's perception of the environment. This sensitivity is not to be achieved through mutual encouragement to be 'more human' or 'caring' with what we already have, but through seeing the 'already there' in a quite different way. Words like 'seeing' and 'reading' must continue to be theorised and worked upon with a method which makes these seemingly innocent words carry the responsibility they deserve.

It is reasonable to assume that the study of communication is the proper area for this kind of work. 'Communication' is a current concern, and an often-used slogan. One of the purposes of this book is to attempt to put into practice theories of reading which have appeared recently in cultural, literary and political studies. The theory of communication which is subscribed to here is one that depends on relative *difference* rather than on the ideal of sameness through 'effective', `skilful' or 'smooth' communication. It attends to the *means* of communication (the media) and the ways in which they represent different positions, types of people and knowledges. Without reducing everything to individual interpretations, or conversely, giving credence to an overarching general theory, it examines what sorts of readings are available, circulating at a given time. The analysis of *what* people are talking about comes from the analysis of the distribution of knowledges in the social arena, which is where they must be. Knowledges don't arise spontaneously in people's heads.

For Krim and myself, seeing the Plains in a new light is to communicate in various ways, and by attending to the *process* of communication, to allow that communication to go on in another place, another position. This process of constant displacement is one that fits in with the way we understand the Aboriginal ideology of the 'dreaming'. There is no basis for seeing the dreaming as a mythological past (as in `dreamtime) while it is alive as a *way of talking*. Paddy Roe, for instance, constantly talks about the *bugarrigarra* as story, as song, as a power he controls and as things to do with *particular places*. To talk *bugarrigarra* about these places is to talk about 'spirits' one cannot see, about the 'rainbow snake' rising up out of springs; it is to talk in a special way which disrupts the uniformity of everyday language. It is a bit like the talk which we call poetry, attributing it with special qualities of transcendence. Could it be that the dreaming is no more than this? Since, in Paddy Roe's case, there is none of that fear which has been associated with 'primitive belief' (no superstitions, no hobgoblins in the dark), only a joy in telling stories and singing songs, then haven't European Australians made a mistake in calling it 'primitive belief', and comparing it unfavourably with 'science'? Someone who talks the discourse of the dreaming deserves to be treated in the same way as a novelist or a poet, but one who comes from a particular culture.

The dreaming is not a set of beliefs which is being lost because it is no longer valid, it is rather a way of talking, of seeing, of knowing, and a set of practices, which is as obtuse, as mysterious and as beautiful as any poetry. Reading its present and public forms as religious, as apolitical, and as the relics of past customs is to deliver it a deathblow. Except where it appears in books, embalmed as it were, it depends on people living in the country, travelling through it and naming it, constantly making new stories and songs.

This book is a record of Paddy Roe's dreaming at its most important nexus: the country itself. Of course, as the spoken voice is transfoirmed into writing and the country then becomes the book, the traveller in turn becomes a reader. Our experience of Roebuck Plains taught us that one can drive along happily only to be brought to a halt by a fence. The only way to go on is on foot, but at that pace a whole different range of things becomes visible. Again, stopping for a while and gazing at the country produces a different effect; one belonging more to the image. In the process of writing, the book became an attempt to repeat the experience of the Plains in its own structure.

This structure seeks to maintain the separate identities of the three authors; their three strands are woven together in a loose kind of way but each remains forever partially ignorant of the purposes and effects of the other's work. We are all 'foreigners'. Krim and I are foreign to the Plains, Paddy is foreign to the book as a European artifact, Paddy and I are foreign to painting, Krim and Paddy are foreign to the sort of writing and philosophy I have adopted to construct a unity or general direction of the book.

When I sought a unifying theme for a book which emphasises place, the movement from one place to the next, I found it in `nomadology', the study of nomadism.[3] One has to admit that this philosophy is rather adventitious; Krim and Paddy were both brought up within so-called nomadic cultures, and this gave us something to talk about. But there is also a gap in discussions about Aboriginal ways of life; it seems that no one has tried to explain what it means to think like a nomad, or what consequences nomadism as a counter-ideology arising in pre-capitalist use of the land might have on Australian life. One would also want to discredit the idea that nomads somehow 'don't belong' to the country because they are not 'settled'. (In South Australia, the ABC weather reports refer to the southern 'settled areas', as if the Pitjantjatjarra nation to the north just isn't there.) One has to bear in mind that a migrating class of European people came a vast distance, completely unsettling themselves, to arrive in Australia and call the locals `nomads'.

More importantly, nomadology is not a general theory, a summary of observations. It is rather a way of looking which is specific (to a place like Roebuck Plains), a way of representing things (in discontinuous fragments, stopping and starting). It is an aesthetic/political stance and is constantly in flight from ideas or practices associated with the singular, the original, the uniform, the central authority, the hierarchy ... without for all that ascribing to any form of anarchy.

It is descriptive, but also analytical and creative. While it might talk about things people do in their travels, it can also be about abstract journeys taking place while one is sitting down: trips in intensity which involve working with a kind of avidity to keep words and images on the move.

It aims to describe practices, ways of living, while avoiding the pretence of describing a *whole* people. In this sense this book is not *about* Aborigines. We have tried to avoid the us-and-them division by, first of all, having three authors, three sources of author-ity, as it were. Also, the focus on reading, on the means of communication, shifts attention away from people or society (the concern of anthropology) and from the linear depiction of events in time (the concern of history).

But in correcting some things, other gaps appear. Women's voices play only a small part in this book; the Aboriginal women's reading of Roebuck Plains, for instance, would no doubt be significantly different. In following Paddy Roe's direction we found, according to tradition, that a strict separation was maintained between `men's business', which seemed to be our lot, and women's cultural activities and experience. The book therefore emerged largely as a gendered object.

The focus on problems of communication and culture has meant leaving other concerns to the side. There is another story to be told about the land which would complement this one; the story of its economic re-development. First the Europeans brought sheep to this country, then cattle, diseases, racial intolerance, violence and alcohol. Within fifty years of first settlement, all the blacks had moved off Roebuck Plains. Now with the country safely in the hands of the white settlers a certain sort of repressive tolerance is returning, one that allows a chink to appear in the anti-Aboriginal armoury. The cultural reconstruction of Roebuck Plains may one day be possible, in ways set out by modern Aboriginal organisations like the National Aboriginal Council, which is working to make the country liveable once more on the basis of Aboriginal land and Aboriginal philosophies.

You are looking at Paddy Roe while he is glancing to his left. Will your gazes evermeet? If they do, will you recognise each other? Will this recognition be based on sameness or difference?

Djila I

1983, 57 cm x 76.5 cm, gouache and pastel on D'Arches paper

Nomadic Writing

The gaze encounters words as if they had strayed to the heart of things, words indicating the way to go and naming the landscape being crossed.

Foucault

The writer can only imitate a gesture that is always anterior, never original. His only power is to mix writings, to counter the ones with the others, in such a way as never to rest on any one of them.

Barthes

The summer vacation was over and instead of going back to the College to teach a new term, I was heading west across the desert towards Perth. Paddy Roe had asked me to write a book about his country and I had bought an old Falcon utility to run around in. In Perth I was to pick up my old friend from Paris, Krim Benterrak, and then we would head north to Broome, pearl town of the Kimberleys.

I hadn't seen either Paddy or Krim since the time of the Broome festival of the previous year. We had sat down on that occasion and talked about doing a book together. Paddy Roe had wanted a record of his country, his home country with which he has the closest links Krim and I were both inspired by what the old man had to say and by the beauty of the intimate link between his words and the constancy of the country itself. Krim was trained in painting in his mother country Morocco and in Paris, where he was a student. He wanted to do more landscape paintings, like the one he had done for the cover of Paddy Roe's first book, *Gularabulu*.4 I wanted to write a book sensitive to Aboriginal understandings of the country, one that wrote nomadically, constantly deferring its authority to other sites and their guardians.

So in making a book about Paddy Roe's country there is no ultimate and unified authority. First there is the existing Aboriginal account and then there is the desire of a man to speak that story. Similarly, there is no landscape authority: there is a tradition of Australian landscape painting and Krim's desire to paint.

There have been many books and there is the desire to make a book communicate something. What are books for? The famous literary critic, I A Richards, had one way of putting it: 'A book is a machine for thinking with'.

A book is like an organic machine in a production line of other machines: conceived in a typewriter, gestated in a publishing house, born on a press, consumed in *the* press, read by people who have been through the schooling machine. It can pick you up in one thinking spot and take you to another one. It's like a ute.

Shortly we arrived in Broome we were called upon to speak to a social club, the 'Coterie'. There were three of us, but Paddy Roe's place had been taken by another friend, Ray Keogh, a musicologist (whose contribution to *Reading the Country* was later to become important). At the Mangrove Motel we all became very relaxed and excited and then gave our little speeches. I took the opportunity to give an account of what the book was to be about. This is what I said:

> *I would like to explain what Krim, Paddy and I are trying to do with this book* Reading the Country. *Most of what I say will have to do with my role in the book which is that of writer, photographer and coordinator of the others' work. What we are mainly interested in doing is bringing together words and images—Paddy's voice, my texts, Krim's paintings, my photographs. All these things represent in different ways, from different positions, the one constant —Roebuck Plains —this is the country we will be 'reading'.*
>
> *Most of us would agree that it is a huge pleasure to write captions to images, or present images in words. This happens at all cultural levels, from the high cultural activity of art criticism, to the popular cultural activity of the slide evening or showing someone the family photo album. In each case the sense of the event of showing is contained neither in the image itself nor in the commentary, but in the particular conjunction of what can be said (or must be said) in relation to that specific image.*
>
> *So this is Paddy Roe's pleasure in showing us his country. He directs our gaze in a certain direction and then supplements this vision with the appropriate words which are his privilege to utter. Then, in turn, Krim constructs a painting*

from what he sees and what is said, and this new image can become the subject of another commentary.

This word-image relation has nothing mystical about it because both words and images are material, material which can be formed into texts. 'Text' is the word which I can use to describe both images and words after they have been worked upon and formed into some sort of shape.

Roebuck Plains itself is not a text, not until it is read or interpreted by someone like Paddy Roe and then produced as an Aboriginal reading of that country. This reading might take the form of spoken narrative (storytelling). The voice is then the material of this text. The voice, which we so often take for granted, is a concrete force: it murmurs, it shouts, it cajoles, it squeals and protests, it bounces along and leaps into song, it groans in our sleep or it makes the little cries of ecstasy which mark our greatest pleasures. In all this, the materiality of the voice cannot be denied, its substance is a vibration which penetrates the bodies of those listening or present. There is no such thing as a neutral voice, a voice which is not in some way composed, like a variation in music, around the basic pattern of what is being said.

And what of writing? Writing is equally a material thing. These tracings on paper, which I am now translating into another medium, the voice, have a different origin, a different form, and different purposes. One follows different sorts of conventions and one derives a different sort of pleasure writing about images than one does speaking about them. In the writing of texts one can stop and think, scratch out sentences, go back and begin again. The texture of writing is the material force. By 'texture' I mean, quite literally, the way the text is woven—in the same way as one says the texture of a fabric. 'The fabric of a text' is equally a phrase which is quite often used to point to just this effect.

Texts are woven—with different colours, if you like—different voices mingling, allusions to someone else's words, citations, different points of view. Texts, like fabrics, are composed of these different colours. The images in this book are similarly materials to be worked upon in ways made possible through the media nvolved. Krim experiments with lines, colours, paint texture, luminosity. For the photography I experiment with camera lenses, angles and the grain of the image.

All this to contribute to one small rectilinear object—a book. An object to be promoted, circulated, sold and read. A *book is a little communicative item which is destined to be shunted around; bought, borrowed, stolen and ending up in places the authors would never have imagined. It is only valuable as long as it is travelling or as long as eyes are travelling across its surfaces. It's like a nomad in the sense that it belongs to a certain territory, yet only lives if it is made to move and to be seen to be going somewhere—perhaps putting on a fine dust jacket to pick up a nice reader, for it is also an object of desire.*

Having given this talk, which announced our presence and purpose in the (white) Broome community, it was then a question of moving out to the country and beginning the work. Krim and I set up camp at Coconut Wells, on Paddy's block of land. Not only do Paddy Roe and Butcher Joe (Nangan) live here, but also various members of Paddy's family at different times. Among the domestic animals were a mob of cats, a little dog and a nanny goat.

At the beginning of a journey, when you are about to cover strange territory, you are always ignorant and you have to rely on the local guides. They are the ones who know the safe tracks as well as the places of danger. And the journey is as much intellectual as it is physical. Krim and I had brought our bodies of course, reasonably intact, but also a certain amount of intellectual baggage, which, it must be admitted, could be of absolutely no use in Aboriginal country.

Paddy Roe said: You want a chair? I always sit on the ground —more better, can't fall down'.

Paddy Roe and his people have their intellectual baggage too, their culture and philosophies. Significantly, these are located *in* the country, the stories and songs are strung out across the Plains and are brought out as one moves along the tracks. Paddy Roe has an expression for the production of this culture: 'We must make these things *move*'.

But we were still sitting in the camp at Coconut Wells. It was the tail end of the wet season and the country was still muddy and too difficult to drive across. This enforced stillness caused me to reflect on the potentially static nature of our project: the production of a white man's artifact, a book. How could I make this thing *move?*

A book has to be a set of traces, words going somewhere. The nomadic reader will then come along afterwards and track things up, deciphering the traces. There will be no general idea of what the whole thing is about, only specific lines to be followed. Singular authority and overarching general theory will be abandoned in favour of local and strategic movements, where one person's story ends the other one takes off. Nomadic writing writes itself; its authority comes from the territory covered, not the person temporarily in charge of the pen. It cannot be imperial (like General Theory) because it has to abandon the traces it leaves behind and anyone can follow them up. But what do they find in the end? The material object, a book which is the product of reading the tracks made across a piece of country. But also an intellectual space made through the essentially nomadic practice of moving from one set of ideas or images towards another set progressively picked up on the way. If this imaginary journey will move closer to Aboriginal understandings of a part of Australia it is not for one person to say. The book can only be a white man's artifact in the end, but Paddy Roe's texts can be read independently (and must be read) as paradoxically *included* in the book, and thus incorporated in the broader culture, but extending before and beyond the covers (already crossing the country before the book was thought of), one word after the other like footsteps: lively spoken words.

These are the words which most clearly and consistently tell of the country. They are set in the context of a Babel of other voices—writings—from the past and present which clamour around and are, in contrast, quite ephemeral. Restricted to particular historical periods, they are the *other* discourses on the country. There will be more to come, following in Paddy Roe's footsteps, or ignoring them. But one ignores the local guide at one's own peril, for he is telling us how to survive in this country, and survival depends not just on the right sort of physical treatment of the country, but also on what one says about it, writes about it, and the images one makes of it.

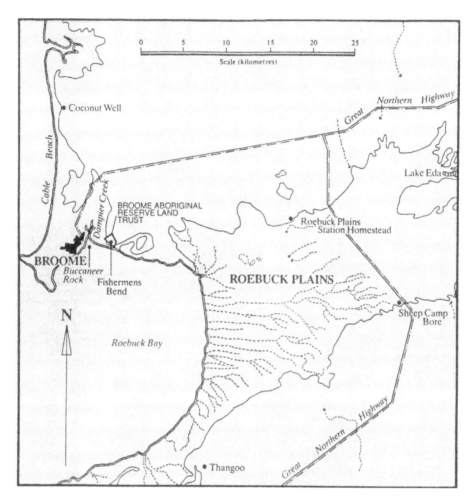

ROEBUCK PLAINS AND BROOME

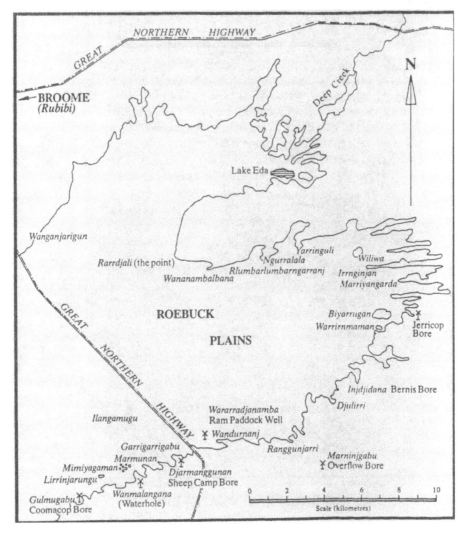

NORTHERN HIGHWAY

GREAT

Deep Creek

← BROOME
(Rubibi)

N

Lake Eda

Wanganjarigun

Rarrdjali (the point)

Yarringuli
Ngurralala
Rlumbarlumbarngarranj
Wananambalbana

Wiliwa
Irrnginjan
Marriyangarda

ROEBUCK

PLAINS

Biyarrugan
Warrirnmaman

Jerricop
Bore

GREAT

NORTHERN

HIGHWAY

Injdjidana Bernis Bore

Djulirri

Ilangamugu

Wararradjanamba
Ram Paddock Well
✗ Wandurnanj

Ranggunjarri

Marninjgabu
✗ Overflow Bore

Garrigarrigabu
Marmunan
Mimiyagaman
Lirrinjarungu

Djarmanggunan
Sheep Camp Bore

Gulmugabu
Coomacop Bore

Wanmalangana
(Waterhole)

0   2   4   6   8   10

Scale (kilometres)

ABORIGINAL PLACE NAMES OF ROEBUCK PLAINS

DISCOVERY

While we were waiting for the country to dry up, Butcher Joe sang a series of songs, the songs which give a musical and poetic reading of the Plains. Each song is associated with a particular place.

When he finished, he had a drink of tea and announced, rather casually, that the old people used to speak of a sailing ship coming across Roebuck Plains while it was under water. Astounded, I question him further. It was just one ship and it appeared long before the white man came to the country. (Could this have been Dampier?) He even insisted that the ship had landed at *Biyarrugan* (see map) and provided two other details which were to concur with European history: it was a three-master, and the sailors had shot at the Aboriginal people. Already an unexpected diversion. I was thrown back on my own resources, so to speak, and while we were waiting for an Aboriginal reading of the country, our first step in the book would be backwards, to white history and its documents. Then it would be sideways to the scientific discourse of geology, another reading of the country.

The discourse of history—the European sort—is largely constructed around important dates and important individuals. Let's indulge ourselves in this sort of reading of the country to see what we can discover.

On the thirtieth day of August 1699, William Dampier was sailing up the north-western coast of Australia in his ship the *Roebuck*. His journal records:

> ... *being in Lat. 18 deg. 21 min. we made Land again, and saw many great Smokes near the shore; and having fair weather and moderate Breezes, I steer 'd in towards it. At 4 in the afternoon I anchor 'd in 8 Fathom Water, clear sand, about 3 Leagues and a half from the Shore. I presently sent my Boat to sound nearer in, and found 10 Fathom about a Mile farther in; and from thence still farther in the Water decreased gradually to 9, 8, 7, and at 2 Mile distance to 6 Fathom. This evening we saw an Eclipse of the Moon ...* [5]

35

Dampier must have made his latitude reading at twelve noon, because the sextant he would have used measures the maximum angle between the sun and the horizon. At that stage he was slightly south of Cape Villaret. Four more hours brisk sailing would have taken him to the bay which is now named after his ship. Whether his boat landed on the beach near the present site of Broome or sailed across a flooded Roebuck Plains, is impossible to determine. But one thing is certain; with the eclipse of the moon he would have had the advantage of king tides, rising as they do as much as ten metres.[6]

As Dampier directed his gaze over this country certain things became visible to him, things he had been trained to look for, or things he had seen in other countries. Dampier left the clues in his journal which would later insert him in history as the first Englishman to make a landing in Australia, but the discourse of his journal is not one of history, it is that of the explorer. As explorer he prefigures colonialist expansion. In his account, certain selections or obsessions reveal an *economic* order of which he is but a tentacle. He is looking for plants that can be exploited, and was not so interested in minerals. He left these for his nineteenth- and twentieth-century descendants:

The land hereabouts was much like the part of New Holland that I formerly described (Vol. 1), 'tis low, but seemingly barricado'd with a long chain of Sand-hills to the Sea, that lets nothing be seen of what is farther within Land. At high Water the Tides rising so high as they do, the Coast shows very low; but when 'tis low Water it seems to be of an indifferent heighth. At low Water-mark the Shore is all Rocky, so that then there is no Landing with a Boat: but at high Water a Boat may come in over these Rocks to the Sandy Bay, which runs all along this Coast. The Land by the Sea for about 5 or 600 yards is a dry Sandy Soil, bearing only Shrubs and Bushes of divers sorts. Some of these had then at this time of Year, yellow flowers or Blossoms, some blue, and some white; most of them with a very fragrant Smell. Some had Fruit like peascods; in each of which there were just ten small peas; I opened many of them but found no more nor less. There are also here some of that sort of Bean which I saw at Rosemary Island: And another sort of small and hard Pulse, growing in Cods also, with little black Eyes like Beans. I know not their Names, but have seen them used often in the East-Indies for weighing Gold; and they make the same use of them at Guinea, as I have heard, where the Women also make Bracelets with them to wear about their Arms. These grow on Bushes; but here is also a Fruit like Beans growing on a creeping sort of

Shrub-like Vine. There was also great plenty of all sorts of Cod-fruit growing on the Sand-hills by the Sea-side, some of them green, some ripe, and some fallen on the Ground: But I could not perceive that any of them had been gathered by the Natives; and might not probably be wholesome Food.

The Land farther in, that is lower than what borders on the Sea, was so much that we saw of it, very plain and even; partly Savannahs, and partly Woodland. The Savannahs bear a sort of thin coarse Grass. The Mould is also a coarser Sand than that by the Sea-side, and in some places 'tis Clay. Here and a great many Rocks in the large Savannah we were in, which are 5 or 6 Foot high, and round at top like a Hay-cock, very remarkable; some red and some white. The Woodland lies farther in Still; whence there were divers sorts of small Trees, scarce any three Foot in circumference; their Bodies 12 or 14 Foot high, with a Head of small Knibs or Boughs. By the sides of the Creeks, especially nigh the Sea, there grow a few black Mangrove-Trees.[7]

Dampier was making these discoverer-type notes on the last day of August in 1699. His men had come ashore and looked for water, but failed to find it. The locals came to observe and 'stood there menacing and threatening of us'. Dampier and his men chased them around, one of the sailors was wounded with a spear and Dampier shot one of the 'New-Hollanders'. For this act, he writes, he was 'very sorry'.

Perhaps the Broome people never forgot the arrival of the sailing ship. I was somewhat surprised when Butcher Joe told me that day that 'the old people bin see sailing ship come up right across plain', but I had no reason to disbelieve him, since other research, in this case from Queensland, shows that Aboriginal popular memory can go back as far as ten thousand years, to a time when the land was differently formed:

It is said that two newly initiated men broke a taboo and so angered the rainbow serpent ... As a result 'the camping place began to change, the earth under the camp roaring like thunder. The wind started to blow down as if a cyclone were coming. The camping place began to twist and crack. While this was happening there was in the sky a red cloud of a hue never seen before. The people tried to run from side to side but were swallowed by a crack which opened in the ground ...'

This was a plausible description of a volcanic eruption. After telling the myth, in 1964, the storyteller remarked that when this happened the country around the lakes was 'not jungle—just open scrub'. In 1968, a dated pollen diagram from the organic sediments of Lake Euramoo by Peter Kershaw (1970) showed, rather surprisingly, that the rainforest in that area is only about 7,600 years old. The formation of the three volcanic lakes took place at least 10,000 years ago.[8]

If the sea did at one stage cover Roebuck Plains, and the *Roebuck*, Dampier 's ship, was anchored near *Biyarrugan* as Butcher Joe claims, then Dampier and his men would have been looking at the country around the south-west side of the Plain where the named places follow the edge of the Plain, as if they were once seaside camps. The occasional shell-midden is still in evidence at *Mimiyagaman*. Would the people have bothered to carry shells the twenty kilometres from Fishermen's Bend *(Garnun)* to *Mimiyagaman?*[9]

Paddy Roe remembers the plains being flooded before; in the wet season, and with a high tide, this can still happen. In the early days when there was a sheep station at *Djarrmanggunan*, the Aboriginal people made a raft out of planks and kerosene tins and poled their way from the station to high ground on the north side of the plain to get supplies.

The 'truth' of history loses its singularity in conflicting accounts. Accuracy of time measurement, as in dates, or their linearity, are no guarantees of truth. What also has to be considered is the way the texts communicate and the purposes they serve. While Aboriginal spoken accounts of history have only recently been taken seriously as leads into Australia's history, that is, historians have begun to consider the possibility of arriving at truth without the support of dates or documents, the tendency is still to go to other mechanisms of truth to validate an historical assertion. The physical sciences can validate history with their instruments of measurement.

With the image of the *Roebuck* sailing the Plains exciting my imagination (maybe there was to be another discovery!) I went to see Dr Eric Lohe at the Shell Metals office in Broome. What I found there was not a 'truth' about the Plains being under water, but another language. Eric kindly offered us another reading of the country. It is an exploratory gaze like Dampier's, but it is one which sees another world in the Plains.

Geology of the
Broome and Roebuck Plains Area
E M Lohe

Regional geological setting

The Broome-Roebuck Plains area is located within a large geological feature known as the Canning Basin, which covers an area of some five hundred thousand square kilometres. It is an intracontinental basin which developed when the older Pre-Cambrian continental crust was down-faulted to form a graben or trough-like structure. The Pre-Cambrian rocks can be seen to the north of the basin in the King Leopold Ranges and the Kimberley Plateau.

Sedimentary rocks which infill the basin form a pile which reaches thirteen thousand metres, but is commonly six thousand metres or less in thickness. Most of these rocks range in age from four hundred and fifty to two hundred and fifty million years before the present (the Ordovician to the Permian Period). A thin veneer of younger sedimentary rocks of mostly two hundred and thirty to sixty-five million years before the present (the Mesozoic age) was also deposited on top of these rocks. The Canning basin thus existed as an active geological structure for a long period of time; more than three hundred and fifty million years.

Widespread lateritisation has occurred throughout the Kimberley region. Laterite is formed by a process of deep weathering of the surface and near-surface rocks, usually during periods of high rainfall and growth of lush vegetation in a tropical or sub-tropical climate. The extensive formation of residual deposits of iron oxides is an important part of this process, and as a result, laterite is characterised by a bright orange-red ferruginous colour at the top of the lateritic profile. Playford et al (1975) [10] noted that the age of the lateritic profile, which is up to fifteen metres thick, is probably Tertiary, but may be as young as early Pleistocene (about 1.8 m.y. B.P. [one million, eight hundred thousand years Before the Present time]).

The youngest deposits of the area are Quaternary in age (ie. younger than 1 8 m.y. B.P.; the Quaternary period is divided into the Pleistocene, as well as the Holocene or recent. The latter represents the last ten thousand years of geological history). The most widely distributed Pleistocene deposit is the distinctive bright red dune sand which occurs throughout much of the Canning Basin. The dunes have been described by Veevers and Wells (1961)[11], Playford et al (1975)[12], and Semeniuk (1980).[13] They are a longitudinal type of dune which forms a series of parallel ridges roughly east-west in orientation. Longitudinal dunes develop as ridges parallel to the direction of the strongest prevailing wind at the time of their formation. The dune ridges, which are up to thirty-two kilometres in length, are a distinctive geographic feature of many parts of the Kimberley region. For example, they are well-developed in the Great Sandy Desert, and also occur in the Broome-Derby area. The dune system is no longer active. The ridges are described as being 'fixed' or stabilised by a cover of vegetation, which includes *Eucalyptus* and *Acacia* shrublands and woodlands.[14] Sheets of aeolian (wind-borne) red sand without a well-defined dune structure also occur in some areas.[15] Semeniuk formally defined the dune deposits as the Mowanjum Sand.[16] The sand which is incorporated into the dunes and sand sheets was possibly derived from the top of the earlier-formed lateritic profile.[17]

Broome-Roebuck Plains area

The oldest rocks cropping out in the Broome area are assigned to the Broome Sandstone, which is early Cretaceous in age (about 130 m.y. B.P.). They are well-exposed at Gantheaume Point, and include footprints of a dinosaur. The formation is comprised of well-bedded, flat-lying and cross-bedded sandstone with minor conglomerate and mudstone. It is one of the youngest units of the Canning Basin.

The top of the Broome Sandstone was lateritised during the Tertiary. It is covered by a variety of Quaternary deposits, particularly the red aeolian sands mentioned above, and mixed alluvial and aeolian deposits, which are of immediate interest here.

The Roebuck Plains form a topographically low area twelve to fifteen kilometres wide and up to thirty-seven kilometres long extending in an east-north-east direction from the coast of Roebuck Bay. It is a distinctive area which stands out on Landsat satellite imagery. The Roebuck Plains include low swampy areas which are characterised by ti-tree vegetation. They are subject to severe inundation during the wet season, and even at the present time the combination of flooding and king tides can apparently cause penetration of tides inland from Roebuck Bay.

On the southern and eastern side, the plains area is surrounded by the Quaternary red aeolian sands and dunes equivalent to the Mowanjum

Formation described earlier. Well-defined dunes extend as ridges into the plains area at its eastern end. The youngest Quaternary sediments under the Roebuck Plains are described as clay, silt, sand, with minor salt deposits, and are considered to have originated in a supratidal mudflat environment. (Gibson & Walton, 1978; Broome 1:250 000 Geological Map.) The Roebuck Plains were, therefore, subject to periodic tidal inundations in the recent geological past.

The fact that tidal flow occurred over Roebuck Plains suggests that mean sea-level was slightly higher in the recent past than it is now. Sealevel has in fact fluctuated considerably in the last twelve thousand years, as Semeniuk's study of the Quaternary deposits of King Sound shows.[18] Tidal deposits in the Derby area which formed above the present sea-level called the Torment Point Sand have been dated to five hundred to one thousand one hundred and ninety years ago by carbon dating of mangrove stumps (Jennings & Coventry, 1973).[19] Although no radiometric data have been obtained from the Roebuck Plains area, the clarity with which the supratidal deposits covering the plains are outlined on Landsat photography suggests that they are geologically quite young. It may therefore be possible to equate them with the Torment Point Sand of the Derby coast.

The general geological evidence suggests that some credence can be given to Aboriginal traditional stories that the sea did penetrate up into the Roebuck Plains area in the past, perhaps only five hundred to a thousand years ago. Carbon dating or organic matter associated with the supratidal deposits would give an indication of their age. Unfortunately, they are poorly exposed or not exposed at all in the flat plains, so that suitable material may be difficult to obtain.

Garrigarrigabu iwarra warra larrayi
PLACE   'heaven'/the other side

indina ima ngaringarindjina yana
she   has gone there   now

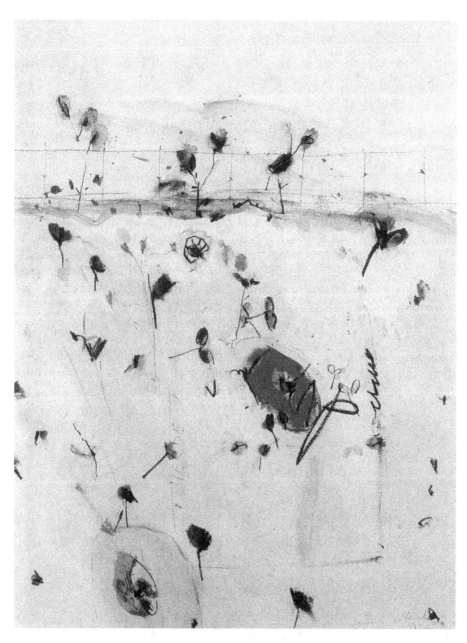

Garrigarrigabu
1983, 57 cm x 76.5 cm, gouache and pastel on D'Arches paper

GARRIGARRIGABU

Our first trip with Paddy Roe and Butcher Joe took us to the eastern side of the Plains, to the Old Sheep Camp. On this southern edge of the Plains the highway cuts right through the place which is traditionally named *Garrigarrigabu*. At this point places on both sides of the road go by this name. This is how Paddy Roe constructed the country as we walked along:

This is all *Garrigarrigabu*   one spring there   one spring right over there   but he's on top this water you know   that's only rainwater that one   he's not a, whatname   proper spring.

See how small this fella bin get? before he that big spring   (Laugh) you can see, all clear, you know[20] an' today he bin get very small   he cover

44

himself   with that grass now   today.
Stephen: Mm.

This is the spring   this is not rainwater.
Stephen: No.
This is spring coming out all the time   might be, four five six years,
seven eight years   no rain   this fella still spring (Laugh) you know
that's the spring   that's *Garrigarrigabu.*

Oh these trees bin here before I born   (Laugh) I born in that hill   that's
the camping ground belong to my old people you know   that hill that's
the hill there   that's the hill I born   there in the bush.
Stephen: Oh, right.

Before they build this house they only had drink outa the, spring   water
you know   old people.
Krim: Your people.

My people before this station built   my people used to, drink water just
out of the   from the springs.
Stephen: Yeah.

Stephen: What's this one?
Well this is not a spring   this is only from rainwater too   that's the old
well   first well they put in   before they built the house.

Krim: Plenty ducks
Ooh everywhere! (Laughs)   we throw boomerang I get four or five we
got-em with boomerang that's true too.

Now this is the old well   when they first put the station they had this
well for drinking.
Krim: The grass here is different.
Couch grass   all couch.
Krim: And this is one here, the other one?
Oh he dry up anytime he's more like a watery[21]   you see this one?
(Squeezes grass)   but no good to eat.

That's the well, you can see the old sheet iron?
Stephen: Yeah.
That one, that's the old sheet iron first well   first old well before the
home was built   station.

Now this place   this is   *Djarrmanggunan   Djarrmanggunan?*
Stephen: Djarrmanggunan   *right here where this well is?*
Aah no, that well is only   somebody bin dig-im only not very long well
I mean when they built the house   this is *Djarrmanggunan* spring
that's the spring.

Now that's the same sorta spring   never go dry.
Stephen: Yeah.
Never go dry   somebody might think he's a dam

46

but he's not a dam he's a spring (Laugh) you know   but now he's got little bit more water in him because   might be bit from rain too   but he should be like the first one we see   he should be like that   you can see the cattle   bin drinkin' all the time   in the dry season you know cattle walk in to get their drink yeah.
Stephen: Is that cattle track there?
Cattle track yeah.
Stephen: Got big foot that one.
Ah Brahman.
Stephen: Oh yeah Brahman.
Oh big big big Brahmans here about that high (Laughter).

This is *Djarrmanggunan* now, proper.
Stephen: Right.
And this station we call-im *Djarrmanggunan* station you know   but this is a *Djarrmanggunan* proper, spring   this one.

We used to make lizard.[22]
(A flock of ducks rises as we approach the springs.)
Little duck   (Laughter) just fly away from here.

Stephen: You used to make things with that, clay.
Eh?
Stephen: You used to make-em?
We used to make-em.
Krim: Mm, snake, everything, kangaroo.
So when he bin grow big, we start then behind mob again[23]   same thing   here (Laugh).
Stephen: Oh, right.

We used to run away from station, you know   boss never see us we hide away here (Laughter)   this was all scrub too   but only sheep country   but today all bullock, you see that's why it keeps more clean all right we better go an' have a look at the old station.

Now all these springs here today that's all my spirit   (Laugh)   'cos I born here   I born 'mongst these *yungurugu   yungurugu* is the rainbow
snake   he hold that water   always never go dry must be something there underneath (Laugh).

Barni, oh[24]   see the water running?
Stephen: Yeah.

That's the overflow   they put that little trough for cattle to drink   that water run right through there   fill all them holes up there for cattle   so they don't need any windmills or anything.

(We drink.)

Good water?
Krim: Mm, beautiful!
Aaah yeah   middle of the heat *more* cold.
Krim: Are you happy to be back here?
Oooh yeeah yes happy to have a look, see the old country (Laugh) you know   oh   I left this country 1923   sixty years.
Krim: Just after the war, the German war.
Ooh? yeah yeah five year after yeah   long time.

Krim: That's a big bird!
Ibis   ibis ibis.
Krim: Ibis.
Ibis yeah (Laugh)   those all ibis   they eat tick   bullock tick   they're

plenty big enough today   ibis these are little duck   they're all right
(Laugh) that's the water bird too they're always in these springs old
springs   nobody live in these places now.

Ngalar ngandin djina buldjarra
Look back   I look back for her blurry vision
ngandi imana djumunbur milili indjargana
dark   go   dust cloud dust in eye   I have

'But I Was Just Like a Swag, Too'

P'lice was gonna pick me up -
well err all the half-caste childrens you know p'lice pick-em-up whole
    lot[25] -
but my mother didn't want to let me go
Krim: And she hide you ...
Yeah I went er well -

When we left sheep station -
they took me out -
when we got -
we got up to the last windmill anyway -
then from there no more windmills -
we camped there[26]
Krim: Right

So
next morning -
old man was still sleeping -
mother making tea -
before sunrise so we can leave the windmill you know -

An' mother look -
we seen the -
he seen dust in the road you know[27]
Krim: Yeah
yeah -
horse and cart road, no motor car those days (Laugh) -

So
when he seen the dust, 'Hello,' he said -
'Must be somebody' -
look, 'Oh, horse -
oh' –

51

p'licemans, six p'licemans -
well one was a p'liceboy -
six p'licemans, er five
Krim: Five
European man, p'liceman you know -
one was er Aboriginal man -
that time -

And er -
i dunno his name too (Laughter) -
my mother call his name -
but I forget -
that fella -

All right, er -
when he see them -
my mother said, 'Hello, this is a p'liceman coming back from La Grange' -
they come back from La Grange, see -
come back -

'Hello,' he said, after -
my mother said, 'What I gonna do with this little boy?' -
so my mother ooh he think about something he tell the old man, Get up
    get up get up,' he said -
(Growl) 'What for,' he -
'P'lice coming' -
ah they took the canvas outa the old man (Laugh) an', 'Come here boy,'
    he said[28] -
so he put me there, 'Lay down' -
rolled me up -
wind me up an' mother was sitting on me like a swag here's a p'liceman
    coming around the corner now -

'Hello,' he said -
'Good Morning' -
an' old fella sitting up just having a drink of tea too -
mm -

'Any piccaninnies?' he asked, you know -
'Any piccaninnies?' -
'No, we got no pic -
nothing' -
'Where you going?' -

'Oh, we goin' walkabout, now, bush' -
'Yeah, all right, goodbye,' he say -
'We can see that, you no got nobody,' but I was there (Laugh)

Krim: No screaming, nothing?
No, no, I know too
Krim: They told you not to
Yeah not to cry or anything -
no matter you get choked up but leave a bit o'room you know
Krim: How old were you then?
About that high I think (Gestures)
Krim: Five, five years?
Four, five -
but I was just like a swag, too[29] -
'nuff fit, you know (Laughter) -
mother was sitting on me -
oh light too, mother sit down, he know

Djarrmanggunan—second sheep camp
1983, 76.5 cm x 57 cm, gouache and pastel on D'Arches paper

There Are Lines ...'

There are lines which are monsters ... A line by itself has
no meaning; a second one is necessary to give expression to
meaning. Important law.

Delacroix.

Krim's painting 'Djarmanggunan—second sheep camp' (facing page),
establishes a sense of place. It seems to describe the arrival of the white
settlers; the two paddocks of the sheep camp huddle together in an extensive landscape. The only line of escape is the tangential fence, a line
which fences off nothing for farming purposes as far as one can see, but
signifies a *beginning* in terms of the painter's project. It connects the
centre of the horizon with the centre of the right-hand side of the frame.
The vertical and the horizontal now swing together along this armature,
the function of which is to point to two initial conventions of landscape
painting; two conventions which Krim will proceed to dismantle in this
series of paintings. First convention for landscape: make a 'window', a
frame through which an area to become the landscape is constructed.
Second convention: trace the horizon.

Now, if one imagines the country as flat, and the frame/window as
vertical, then the fence which connects the two, and is holding them
apart, is in an interesting position. If one flattened the frame down on
top of the sheep camp, the 'fence' might break off from the frame at its
closest point to the viewer and either collapse on top of the sheep camp,
dividing the painting in two vertical halves (without a sky), or it would
fly out and poke the viewer in the eye.

The second possibility is excessive. It goes beyond the bounds of art
criticism (except that this writing too infrequently warns the viewing
subject of the dangers in looking at paintings).

The first takes away the sky, which is where the painting begins; as
a landscape, since this is the part without land, and where the painter begins his work with the first wash of colour spreading across this

55

northern part of the paper. In the composition of the painting this is the first movement, the *overture* both in relation to colour and to form. The main part (main course) of the composition is the country itself. It is the body, or what Krim calls the 'belly' of the painting.

Trees erupt from the surface of the canvas; they are not placed there, one must admit, because the exuberant colours (orange, apricot, cherry—offset by a reluctant green) vacillate in a complex relation to the central area of the station. The station paddocks are encircled by ambiguous fences—they could be trees alone. There must be a fence there somewhere, because this station is the reason for that other tangential fence out on its own, like the station in the landscape. While that fence *divides* a conceptual space, the station fences just *contain* a space, a space of habitation, of sitting, of settling in fact—which is what the whites are doing there.

So the trees come back to the station which they never even left. There are rows of three or four in the country, just as there are in the station. Krim is not so easily convinced by ideas which say that settling, as such, radically changes the landscape. They are in a continual process of encroachment on each other. This is the body, the main text of this first statement in paint.

But did I forget the station fence, the fence of the home paddock? It is there, of course, in red, covering a brown oval with a pink nipple in the square paddock. In the circular paddock there is a green patch of cultivation, of growth. This garden is the outer paddock. Above it is the more dense inner paddock whose centrality is confirmed in its repetition of the square form of the canvas. In vain we look for a homestead; maybe there's a bower shed denuded of its cover. What we do find is the brown oval covered by the red grid of the barbed wire fence.

This constitutes a symbolic statement of the concluding part of the composition in which our themes are reunited. The fence becomes symbolic, actual people are absent, and a strange series of blue trees line up as the product of that brown oval (with the pink nipple). It is an old spring, of course, the *raison d'être* of all settlement, the permanent water which is the source of life and agriculture. Its lushness is still being sucked up into the blue of the trees, and the source of this goodness is the still-damp centre of the soak itself. This moisture is never too far underground, since it emerges at other points in the landscape inspiring other trees to turn blue.

To the left of the outer paddock is a satellite spring, clear-blue and virgin, a symbol of regeneration and youth. But let's call a halt here, before exhausting our themes: other paintings in the following pages will tell us more about fences, trees, colours, springs, Roebuck Plains and, of course, landscape painting.

Djarrmanggunan gimbandjina wirrilji-wirri
PLACE *balangan* turns around   willy-willy

barninbal 'wokok' indjina-yana
large tadpole 'croak' he said

Story From *Djarrmanggunan*

Did I tell you about that one man bin run away with the woman[30] -
from Mt Anderson? [31]
Stephen: Not Duegara[32]
No no (Laugh) -
oh mighta tell that 'nother bloke -
I musta tell that other bloke -

But we was camping in the woolshed
Stephen: Mm
That's shearing shed you know woolshed -
oh big house

So we got in there -
raintime -
so big rain come - -
biig rain, no cyclone -
or anything but big rain -
an' he bin raining for week -
big rain aall the time -

Stop us from making fire stop us from coming to get our tucker from
    kitchen (Laugh) -
but we come, old people go through, young people you know - -

So that oldfella from Mt Anderson -
he steal his woman this fella steal his woman -
from Mt Anderson -

So that oldfella from Mt Anderson he, hee -
he sent snake for him -
from his country -

'Cos he's a *maban* too
Stephen: Yeah
That fella -

Eeer *yungurugu* -
this rainbow snake *yungurugu* we call-im that one now, only *yungurugu*
    old man (Laugh) -
yeah
Stephen: Yeah
Only *yungurugu* -

So when that *yungurugu* bin come that rainy day -
he went 'round that he find that, man and woman inside there weee, we
    was all together inside -
so that snake went 'round and 'round inside you know he coil himself
    in the house[33] - -
(Soft) yeah -

He was going to drown that place (Laugh) -
yeah, one side -
we can hear night time: *tung tung, tung tung tung tung* eeeer you know
    timber breaking
Stephen: Mm
(Laugh)

Floor -
went down -

'Hello hello what's goin' on?' -
so we put the lights on we only had old eeeer lights eer we
    used to make-em outa grease (Laughter) you know - -
so we look 'Oh the timber broken, one end is gone, finish' -
the berandah is about that high -
you know -
and one end went FINISH, about that much -
if we didn't (Laugh) find out -

So we wake one man up -
that's my brother -
one fella he's *maban* too -
when he get up, oh! too late -
but these fellas bin already up
this lot

Stephen: Er gardiya? *er no*[34]
Noo the *yungurugu* -
They know the stranger there
they all up -
(Laugh) -
all these springs -
all up -

They wanta, chase that fella out -
that's the strange snake[35] -
but they (Laugh) come over the mouth, you know get up right up
Stephen: Mm
Right up in the air - -

So we get this man to have a look, 'Oh' -
he look, oh all the old old fellas bin get up -

They're my spirits (Laugh)
Stephen: What do they look like?
Couldn't see 'em (Laugh) -
it's only man can see it is the *maban* - -
he got, one more eye, better than we got[36]
Stephen: Mm
(Laugh) You know?
Stephen: Yeah
Mm -
he can see long -
right up to La Grange -
with his eye -
(Laugh) -
see -
it's a thing like that, *maban* -

So he put-em down whole lot -

All right -
this fella gone -
finish they hunt-im out he's gone - -
THESE fellas hunt-im out
Stephen: Mm
Snake and snake -
Yungurugu, yungurugu we call-im -

60

I don't know what they look like might be like a, camel or -
(Laughter) might be like a dragon or we don't know
Stephen: Mm

Seee we don't know what *yungurugu* is -
it's only man know is *maban* man - -
So we get up in the morning -
'Hello,' we get up -
aall these trees all these big big trees -
it's like fire bin through - - -
more, this kind time[37] it's all finish burn aall the leaves an' all burn -

But we know what for -
we know -

Because this one burn -
you see -
when they get up -
his back one burn
this is like a glass fire[38] -
(Laugh) -
mamarrarra you know this one we call-im -

Just like a fire -
Just like a eeeer might put er (Laugh) you know if you stand over there
    and I put a glass on you you know with the sun -
he burn you (Laugh) -
it's a thing like that -
ooh leaves all fall off next (Laugh) -
finish -
fire -

But we know -
that's this part (Laugh) -
in this country now - -
I know it's very hard to b'lieve you know but er it's there -
so -
that's why we say sometimes - -
well nobody else can get-im it's only -
must be country man - -

But they very good to us too -
they're not bad you know country, things -

other country things good for them too, bad for yunmi - -
an' here if it's my country well it's good for country man -
but no good for him -
because when they smell-em too -
straightaway -
mm -

But today too many cloud you know -
if this is all clear - -
but this is not the place -
this is where I born -

But he got more bad one other side[39] -
he bring cyclone -
oh just a little cyclone 'null to (Laugh) mess around with this fella who
    bin there (Laugh) -
lightning strike, rain -
oh just about lift a motor car up too -
(Laugh) -

And this is the place

I musta tell that other fella.

Oh he didn't put him down or anything but I just told-im about the
story what the *yungurugu* means you know he didn't know what the
yungurugu I'm talking about   well I s'pose still too today you people
don't understand what I'm talking about you know it's a *yungurugu*
  if
somebody tell me just the name an' all that because (Laugh)   eer I
might think, 'What is this—?'   you know   if somebody else tell me
something   well that's why.

But this is a   that's why these springs   permanent springs   you
know
from *bugarrigarra*   he bin like that water snakes never go 'way
from this part of the country.
Stephen: Yeah.
Stay here   because   it's only three people really born in this
country.

I was the first one to born in this country so this is all my spirit.

But the other two born just after me but they got nothing   you know.
Krim: You were first.
I first   in this country so spirits all mine   these two people only bin born they bin come from somewhere you know mother and father   not very long.
Stephen: This is Yawur country?
All Yawur country   I was born here in middle of Yawur (Laugh).

When the station was here you know but I'm the first man to born, one boy in this station   in these springs.

Stephen: But it didn't matter that you were Nyigina?
No   my people come to live in this country to die.
Stephen: Mm.
Mother and Father you know.
Stephen: Yeah.
My people come from Nyigina country young time and they come to this place, so I born here.
Stephen: This is your country.
Yawur country but Nyigina girl got married into er   Yawur people.
Stephen: Oh yes.
Yawur people didn't have any girls left in this country   everybody took-em.[40]

Stephen: So Nyigina girls came here.
Nyigina girls came and that was their promise then.
Stephen: Mm.
But girls come from   they're born in 'nother place.

So they got married into Yawur people   Yawur Djaberdjaber Nyul-Nyul ah   not Nyul-Nyul ah   Wumbal Djugun all them people   Garadjari too.

Oh they had some waterholes other side   other side of this hill now waterholes other side   an' all the other springs were all that way too.

Stephen: We'll go there later.
We might go next time when we get the key   that's the fence now run you know   we'll have to see that boss I'll ask-im then but we been here anyhow he don't know   if he see us well we just tell-im too I just tell-im.
Krim: Mm.
What we doin' here   oh he don't mind he's good bloke.

63

No cattle here too.
Krim: Yeah, they're there.
You see them?
Krim: Yeah.
Yeah? (Laugh)   oh yeah right out there yeah   oh well that's good we
never kill anything (Laughter).

TRIBAL AREAS OF THE WEST KIMBERLEY

Map adapted from Tindale, N.
Aboriginal Tribes Australia
ANU Press, Canberra, 1974

The Song in the Story

Each Aboriginal story has its moments in which an animal noise is imitated, or the sound of a windmill, or the song belonging to one of the characters. These mimetic moments are the central point of access for the listener, the surprising moments when language is put aside and the illusion of being there is complete. Around them, the framework of the story is built: the dialogues of the characters, the narrator's voice, the gestures of sand drawing or direction which illustrate the story and firmly place it in its specific context, the laughter of narrator and audience which bursts through the mimetic illusion and thus constitutes the pleasure of the event.

Songs usually fall into two major categories, ones 'given' by the dreaming, *bugarrigarra,* and those invented by singers, *djabi* and *lilyin.* This latter sort has been compared by Paddy Roe to the songs of popular Country and Western singers like Slim Dusty; it's just for entertainment.

Djabi songs, found throughout the North-West, are the subject of a book by C G von Brandenstein.[41] *Lilyin* songs are confined to the Broome area. They have four or five 'lines' of text whereas *djabi* usually only have two. These textual units—verses, are repeated over and over with diminuendo and perhaps a chorus if sung in company. What is normally called a song cycle is the progression, song by song, along a given track in the country, from place to place. When there is a chorus, it follows the main singer, repeating his verses, rising in song after his voice has died away and fading as his voice rises again. This song-dialogue is called 'tracking'.

For many years Butcher Joe has led people in song like this, and he has constructed a song-cycle called his *nulu*. Some of these songs appear in this book while others belong to other cycles and tracks crossing the Plains at different points. Butcher Joe attributes these songs to a figure which European poets used to call their muse. In Butcher Joe's case it is the spirit of his mother's sister who appears in his dreams as a *balangan* (spirit of the dead), taps him on the shoulder and gives him the song (sleeping near Butcher Joe can be a problem because he can wake in the middle of the night singing a song in order to 'get it down'). A drawing was made by Butcher Joe to illustrate this event. The pelican *(mayiarda)* is a major figure in Butcher Joe's *nulu*. The dancing man has the head-dress and body

Decoration appropriate to, and imitating, the pelican. These all come from the spirit in Butcher Joe's dream. She is also the source for the Roebuck Plains songs, the songs are in fact her voice still speaking from the Plains while Butcher Joe is merely the vehicle for that voice.

Presented with line-by-line translations, these songs are a long way from being understood in all their significance. To provide versions of

translations, in the free-verse form that Western readers would understand, is only to hint at their possibilities. If there are two lines, and neither comes first—they just turn around each other, a small cycle within a
larger one—where does the meaning begin? At what point can one begin
to translate, for instance, the *Rarrdjali* song? (page 160.)

> At *Rarrdjali*
> the sun rises
> and a bird sings:
> 'djiburr-djiburr'

Or:

> 'Djiburr-djiburr'
> sings a bird
> at *Rarrdjali*
> in the morning

And is there only one or are there many interpretations? Are the many
interpretations but variations on a single theme?

> At *Rarrdjali*
> the bird sings
> the sun rise
> 'djiburr-djiburr'

Or:

> At *Rarrdjali*
> the sun rise
> is the bird singing
> ' djiburr-djiburr '

The process of translating a song with Butcher Joe and Paddy Roe is
a process of building a story around the song, a story being the next best
thing to the complex poetry of the song, a narrative pleasure supplanting
the musical and poetic pleasure, closing its arms around it while still the
song struggles to break free. The story that follows, told on completion
of Butcher Joe's singing, tells how a countryman made up a *lilyin* song
about Paddy Roe and an emu.

> *Nganggali garra winangga ma*
> *nambangga biya djinggirrin yanga*
> *nilanga labalja buru binbirrin birri*
>
> *Nganggali garra winangga ma*
> *nambangga biya djinggirrin yanga*
> *nilanga la ...*

Nimirrin mirri malanggan indja
bindjiga bindjiga gangidja gadja
yalirin njanjaya gunaga li
gandjangala madju
nimirrin mirri ...

Nganggali garra wingangga ma
nambangga biya djinggirrin yanga
nilanga labalja buru binbirrin birri

Nganggali garra djinggirrin yanga ...

That one emu.

Butcher Joe: 'You fella make fun out of me,' that emu say (Laugh).
I bin killing bullock.
Butcher Joe: 'Stop there, don't come more close,' he tell-im Paddy but
Paddy want to give-im help, you see, that emu (Makes 'emu' hissing
noise) *he go, you know.*

He wanted to get through the barb wire fence   but I see that emu walking he try to get through so I come along and, give-im a help   I open
the fence, I grab-im and put-im through the fence   and from other side
he look me.

But the other fella was   the other fella bin thinkin about now   one of
my bloke too he was killing   but he's a singer too he made corroborees,
Lilyin.

Krim: Mm (Laugh).

This fella you know   'I gonna make *lilyin* outa that too'   (Laughter) he
say, you know   he's getting bullock and he watching me too   all right
he say   next time he made a song, now.
Butcher Joe: Paddy give him a big help, you see   now outside he free
(Makes 'emu' hissing noise).
(Laughter.)
But I bin help 'im through the barbed wire, I put-im through and he
went other side
Stephen: Ah, that's a song about you then.
Yeah me (Chuckling).

When he bin come back he bin sing for me then, all of that man, you know   'Aah', I know straightaway.

Well my people bin playing card   in that boab tree   I show you that
boab tree tomorrow when we go in you know   my people bin playing
card.

And he can hear these fellas laughing too in card, you know, play
'Hello,' he say, 'Might be they make a fun of me'   just like that fella
say you know, err.
Butcher Joe: That err, Djaber-djaber.
He listening   just like he listening:

> *nganggali garra winangga ma*
> *nambanga 'biya'*

somebody bin sing out 'pair', they bin playing poker, that time
(Laughter)   you know   *nambangga biya 'biya',* he say, 'pair'   that
lot talking   but nothing you know he don't know English (Laugh)
emu, you know, that emu talking.
Stephen: Ooh, yeah.
Yeah (Sings)

> *nganggali garra winangga ma*
> *nambanga 'biya'*
> *djinggerrin yanga*
> *nilanga labalja buru*

'I'd like to come up see you fellas'   but (Sings)

> *nganggali garra winangga ma*
> *nambanga*

'Wait I might knock you down,' he tell me (Laughter)   he tell me from
other side, you know (Laugh)   yeah, he say.
Krim: That's a good story.
(Sings)

> *yalirrin njanjaya gunaga li*
> *gandjangala madju*

Gandjangala madju I might   'You go back I might knock you down',
he tell me you know (Laughter) if I want, I break his neck (Hilarity)
but I saved him   (Laugh) you know.
Stephen: That emu heard them call 'pair'?
Card, yeah.
Stephen: Pair?
Pair.
Stephen: Why did he think that was making fun of him?

Somebody was laughing.
Stephen: Ooh.
Same time in the card, playing card you know they make fun.
Krim: Yeah.
To themself.

They didn't see him!   they didn't see him   they playing card   they didn't see-im   only I seen-im.

An' I want to put-im through the fence because he might get caught in the barb wire you know   save his life.
Stephen: He was already getting stuck.
Eh?
Stephen: He was already getting stuck.
He getting stuck already an' I come up an put-im   lift the wire up, put-im through.

All right   but he say   'You didn't grab me   you better go back I might knock you down,' (Laughter) he tell me.
(Sings)

   gunaga li
   gandjangala ma ...

He tell me, 'I might knock you down' (Laughter)   oh he was quiet too, you know, he never kick, or anything (Laugh) I s'pose he was frightened too he wanted to get through (Laugh).

Oh this is only just the songs you know.

A considerable amount of money has been made by people taking photographs of Aborigines. How much did people like Butcher Joe get paid?

Always Already Writing

Speech and writing have always been understood as different forms that language can take. These different forms are valued differently, and there are quite a few prejudices which have been handed down in the traditions of Western thought about these things.

One of these causes us to over-value literacy and hence induce shame and stigma for those of us who are 'illiterate'. In this fragment I shall argue that 'illiteracy' is a misused word, that those people considered 'illiterate' have always been reading or writing in the broad sense, and may only be ignorant of one set of techniques—reading and writing script.

It seems obvious that speech was invented before writing. As far as we know, speech has always been a part of human societies. Writing, for example cuneiform script, hieroglyphics, ideograms (characters) and alphabetic script, is a relatively recent invention that has been noticed to the extent that it has endured as inscriptions in very old stones from the Middle East and Southern Europe. But what if people have been 'writing'—making meaningful traces—as long as they have been speaking? Take, for example, a beautiful Chinese character:

It is Shu, meaning 'to write' or 'book'.[42] In use up until the character reforms of 1956, the ancient Chinese picture-effect of a hand holding a brush poised over paper can be discerned. It represents a whole word, and is not composed of segments in combination which more-or-less stand for sounds, like the alphabetic script.

Alphabetic script is in no way superior to this form of representing meaning. The two function in different ways, and serve different purposes. It is easier to organise English-Chinese dictionaries than it is to do the reverse. The Chinese-English dictionary has to be organised according to the sound of the word. On the other hand the Chinese character is *both* an image and a word—it gives a total meaning effect added to which is the gestural aesthetic effect or the 'flair' with which the character is drawn. Alphabetic scripts also have the possibility of signifying things other than the meanings of the words. This possibility makes the jobs of printers interesting and those of handwriting experts possible.

But even in picture writing each character can have a trace in common in which the meaning is based. This is called the radical.

The sweeping trace which these three characters have in common is the radical which means 'to walk' or 'go towards'. It is gestured graphically; the human figure on the left finds a path stretching to the right, a path which disappears into those fine traces of the brush which are the calligrapher's last gesture, a turn of the wrist. The first is *Dao*, 'a path' or 'a philosophy'. The second is the verb 'to chase', *Zhui* and the third is *Ji*, 'a trace, mark or footprint'. The nomadism of Chinese characters. Given that, when someone is trained to read, any sort of script is decipherable, then it would be foolish to say that the alphabetic script is the best. And further, given that one is often led to believe that there is more 'behind' the words than meets the eye, then how much material is *assumed* when a given trace (word, character) is said to represent a certain chunk of meaning?

The answer to this might be that writing codes are culturally specific and so are the trainings in reading them. Certain modes of reading are culturally produced and always reproduce meanings which are current in a culture, and exclude those which are not current. In this sense reading and writing have much in common, in the sense that they are both

74

active reworkings of texts which are always already written in some adjacent context.

Now when Paddy Roe makes a trace in the sand (see photograph, page 75) and then erases it when he has finished his story, doesn't that trace constitute writing because it is a material trace which conventionally represents something in the real world (Roebuck Plains)? (Of course, since Derrida's work we know that writing doesn't represent, in the sense of *substituting for,* 'the real'. It obeys its own logic, a logic to which neither 'thought' nor 'reality' are standing in any relation of priority.) Paddy Roe's writing is an abstract signifying system of lines, dots, circles and so on. His culture has insignia which represent everything of importance to it: clans, families, movements of people, classical myths and recent events, animals, seasons, plant life and the layout of the country. Do we fail to call it writing because it is kept from white people or because it is erased and redrawn during the telling of stories? Must a trace *endure* to qualify as writing?

A better word for Paddy Roe than 'illiterate', with all its bad connotations, would be the French *analphabète*—someone who doesn't know one particular Western system of writing. Most of us are illiterate in Paddy Roe's writing and the knowledge of the culture which supports it.

Writing, in Western European culture, is not always a key to liberation and self-expression. In spite of widespread education, writing is still a medium of communication used by only a small elite. Most people's writing is limited to quick notes or signatures. The formation of the writing individual has been linked with a number of disciplinary techniques for controlling, supervising, examining and reproducing individuals for the workforce. Michel Foucault has given an account of the 'correct training' which produces these individuals and which concentrates to a great extent on disciplining the body which writes:

> Good handwriting, for example, presupposes a gymnastics— a whole routine whose rigorous code invests the body in its entirety, from the points of the feet to the tip of the index finger. The pupils must always 'hold their bodies erect, somewhat turned and free on the left side, slightly inclined; so that, with the elbow placed on the table, the chin can be rested upon the hand unless this were to interfere with the view; the left leg must be somewhat more forward under the table than the right. A distance of two fingers must be left between the body and the table; for not only does one write with more alertness, but nothing is more harmful to the health than to acquire the habit of pressing one stomach against the table; the part of the left arm from the elbow to the hand must be placed on the table. The right arm must be at a distance from the body of

about three fingers and be about five fingers from the table, on which it must rest lightly. The teacher will place the pupils in the posture that they should maintain when writing, and will correct it either by sign or otherwise, when they change this position.[43]

Notions of freedom or self-expression of the writer might have to be re-examined one day in the light of such descriptions of the disciplines involved in learning to write. Are they a necessary aspect of learning? Where does the desire to write come from, given those learning conditions?

Speech has equally been tied to a regime of repression rather than one of pleasure (I am thinking of the typical elocution class). It is repressive because speech is still condemned or praised in Australia to the extent that in conforms to that authoritarian upper-class English model. The effects of speech trainings may be even more complex and diverse than those of writing. We are torn between exhortations to be 'natural' in our speech and demands to be 'correct'. Speech is either the minor of our individuality or the badge of our authority. In relation to writing speech is still seen as being more primary, originary and closest to thought, as if it weren't just one medium within the conventional medium of a language shared by all. But spoken language, like Paddy Roe's writing, traces an arc in the medium of sound waves before disappearing in minute echoes. It inscribes or gestures meanings in its lilting and grinding, growling or stuttering. These traces of meaning are coded (perhaps with individual 'flairs') so that they can be 'read' by the listener. Speech does not have the special privilege over writing of being able to magically transfer thoughts from one mind to another. We are always using some medium to make some trace, perhaps with an intention to indicate things to others who recognise the trace. But often we leave these traces unconsciously like a lizard scuttling across the sand. It has left a writing which says very clearly: 'I am *barni*, going this way'. People writing English leave themselves open in the same way. They can be tracked down as individuals cohering to a particular set of Western European beliefs.

But how can you tell which way they are going? How do you know if reading this or that set of traces will enhance your survival or give you pleasure?

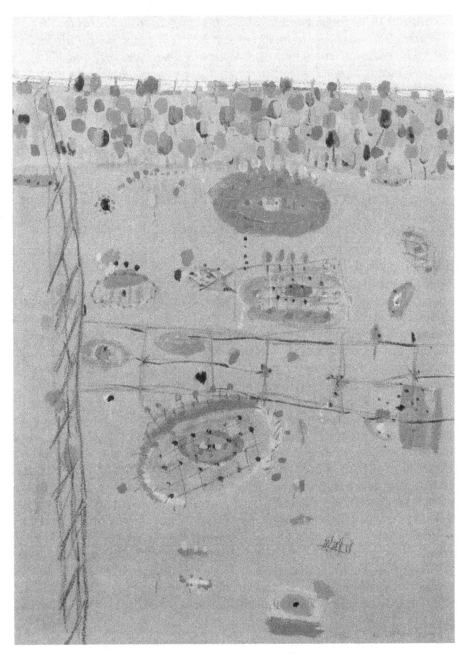

Lirrinyanungu
1983, 76.5 cm x 57 cm, gouache and pastel on D'Arches paper.

The Key to the Country

The fences, gates, buildings and windmills all proclaim one thing about Roebuck Plains which we have neglected to mention: it is owned by someone. If one wants to drive through the country one comes up against the barrier of the boundary fences which have gates with locks. These cut across the tracks Paddy Roe's people used to follow. Short of destroying these fences, the only way to gain access to the country is to drive to the homestead to ask the manager or owner for a key. We did this on several occasions, Paddy Roe bringing a diplomatic boomerang: a metaphorical key perhaps, one that would 'unlock' any opposition from the station people.

Language barriers. What is the password?

This is the quite practical aspect of getting in a position to know the country—having a look at it, but there is a more significant way of gaining knowledge about the country and that is to start by seeing the 'key' as *communication*.

We have already done this by talking with people and seeing the diversity of their different readings of the country. We have learnt that rather than any one of them being absolutely right there is a range of purposes, economic or otherwise, to which each reading offers up its services. The reading becomes the commonsense of the purpose, so that a geological reading of the country stands in a quite 'natural' relationship to the purpose of mining. Each reading thus produces a partial knowledge of the country, and using the reading is the *only* way to gain access to that knowledge; the country does not offer up the fullness of its meaning to the receptive individual as some romantics and spiritualists would have us believe.

Listening to Paddy Roe, one is astounded by the range of his knowledge of the country. What appears between the pages of this book is but a fraction of what he chose to tell us. Traditional secret material is absent; it is only circulated among his own people and is not for public consumption. His knowledge covers the areas we call history, botany, medicine, biology, meteorology, religion, sociology, politics ... I baulked at the idea of trying to record everything he knows. Besides, academics from different disciplines have consulted with him regularly over the past twenty or thirty years; this information must be available somewhere.[44] If one wanted to give priority to any reading at all, it would have to be Paddy Roe's because of the historical depth of his knowledge, and the range of areas which it encompasses.

What then is the strategy for listening to him? How is the communicative key shaped? I could come to him as an economist and then only 'hear' what he has to say about the exchange of goods. Similarly anthropologists have particular listening strategies, as do linguists. There is always a mass of material which they fail to record because it doesn't fit the categories which shape their disciplines. In the Aboriginal-White encounter there are often long silences, an absence of words which speaks of the lack of common ground between Aboriginal discourses and White discourses. Perhaps it is important to record these silences also as we head out from Roebuck Plains Station with the key to the gate which will take us further east from the Old Sheep Camp.

K5 International

(Car starts.)

                        Mmm   I s'pose we better go back that way.

Stephen: Here?
Oh yeah   he all right.

         Yeah that cloud musta come
               through that way
                       rain   you know.

Here this rain coming again see?

    pouring here and there, rain rain.
Stephen: Yeah.

               Little bit here and there, sprinkling
this one coming back again

           it's raining a bit here and here musta gone straight across.

(Car swings out onto the Broome-Derby road.)
Stephen: Nothing.
Nothing.

I left a old International truck here one time   International truck
          I left him for good.
Stephen: What, on this road?
Yeah, they took everything out of him.
Stephen: Same one there?
Same one
I used to go for
          with the windmills.
Stephen: Ah.

I got bogged down one time
so we bought 'nother International
so we tip that old thing over and get the parts off him for the other one.

Old, wartime job   army truck too
       K5 they call it then, K5 International

I used to do all my jobs, 'round the windmills.

Stephen: This side too, Roebuck Plains?
All that one (Indicates south side).
Stephen: This side too?
No only all this way   no windmills this way
    only three up there, four
         in the station
other side of sheep camp, ooh about twenty-seven of them.

They all went down on the cyclone
                          got 'em all up again.

That country all like clay, country, you know, clay
very sticky.
Stephen: All of the country?
                      Plain, yeah.

Little rain, big rain, same
not very small rain but
little bit smaller than big rain, you know?

SOURCES

I am walking on my dream.
                    Paddy Roe.

Paddy Roe is a rain prophet—he knows the movements of clouds, and whether they are bringing rain; he can predict the appearance of cyclones, and knows about the kinship between the Rainbow Snake *(yungurugu)* and the heavy rain which drowns people.

If you break the grass growing out of the 'boss' spring at *Mimiyagaman* (this grass is the snake's goatee beard), the spirit snake is offended and will drench you with rain wherever you may go. In one extreme case, and this is Butcher Joe's dream, a kind of churning, coiling quicksand swallowed up a whole group of people who cooked kangaroo in the wrong place. Then the *maban* men killed the snake by swallowing hair string made from their beards, passing it through their bodies and out of their nether orifices which increased its size, then attaching it to (and coiling it up with) the snake so that they both transformed into each other. The Snake, the Beard, the Source and the Prophet: these are the ingredients of the Roebuck Plains water dream.

In very recent times a machine has made an appearance in the landscape: the windmill. It is easy to see how such a machine could capture the imagination of a man dreaming about water; Paddy Roe became an expert on windmills. He and his team resurrected nearly all of the Roebuck Plains windmills when they blew down one year in a cyclone. When the wind is less strong, it is linked by this machine to the sources of water under the ground. (Paddy knows where these are; he is often employed as a water-diviner.) Troughs and windmills now inhabit the landscape replacing the *djarlbunguru*—the traditional hollow-log wells. But the dream about water is unperturbed, as the following narrative called 'Making rain' shows.

But let us turn first to a myth of another culture, the imperialist one. In his essay on the origins of language, Rousseau (that great champion of the romance of the 'noble savage') discovers the *source*. The source becomes the origin of everything: language, love, fire, industry:

> *In the arid places where water could be had only from wells, people had to rejoin one another to sink the wells, or at least to agree upon their use. Such must have been the origin of societies and languages in warm countries.*
>
> *This is where the first ties were formed among families: there were the first rendezvous of the two sexes. Girls would come to seek water for the household, young men would come to water their herds. Their eyes, accustomed to the same sights since infancy, began to see with increased pleasure. The heart is moved by these novel objects: an unknown attraction renders it less savage; it feels pleasure at not being alone. Imperceptibly, water becomes more necessary. The livestock become thirsty more often. One would arrive in haste, and leave with regret. In that happy age when nothing marked the hours, nothing would oblige one to count them; the only measure of time would be the alternation of amusement and boredom. Under old oaks, conquerors of the years, an ardent youth will gradually lose its ferocity. Little by little, they become less shy with each other. In trying to make oneself understood, one learns to explain oneself. There too original festivals developed. Feet skipped with joy, earnest gestures no longer sufficed; the voice accompanied them in impassioned accents: pleasure and desire mingled and were felt together. There at last was the true cradle of nations: from the pure crystal of the fountains, flowed the first fires of love.* [45]

A delightful romance, but a false one. The search for origins is futile. Where did the nomadic herdsmen come from, if not their parents? And their parents had also exchanged words. There are no beginnings, only the desire to search for them brought about by static knowledges, practices and metaphors. People try, for instance, to fix their origin in an important ancestor by constructing family 'trees'. This kind of practice reinforces beliefs in the power of bloodlines and the importance of keeping families and races 'pure'; a dangerous belief which was scandalised by Darwin's *On the Origin of Species* since this book gave Man his origin in the ape.

The powerful metaphor of the *tree* and the *root* has given us all sorts of anti-nomadic understandings, like modern European languages having their 'origins' in Latin and Sanskrit. It even makes modern linguists in Australia obsessed with the search for *the* original Aboriginal language: Proto-Australian. This sort of language study represents a flight away from problems associated with how people can write and talk in the present; how to write Aboriginal history, for instance, and how best to create Aboriginal literature.

If the tree is to be retained at all as a metaphor, it should perhaps be viewed from above; with roots and branches fanning out in all directions from the centre, their meeting place. The tree is then like strands of life collecting together around a source of water; it is a turbulent multiplicity and life flows both ways along its strands, the roots having no more of 'the origin' about them than the leaves.

Nomads, also, flow in both directions between sources. These springs are successive and don't reduce to the same thing each time one arrives in a place. Different sorts of activity occur at these multiple centres and each spring has its song, ritual and set of stories. Activity is contingent upon the place, stories come to mind as one moves towards the site at which they can be repeated and there isn't an all-encompassing story. This contingency of storytelling was recognised by Edgar Allen Poe, in his story 'A Descent into the Maelstrom':

> *You must get over these fancies, said the guide, for I have brought you here that you might have the best possible view of the scene of that event I mentioned—and to tell you the story with the spot just under your eye.*[46]

Aboriginal storytellers have a similar policy. If one is not prepared to take the trouble to go to the place, then its story can only be given as a short version. If one expects, following Western tradition, that each person will be the sole source of a story, then one will be surprised to find a contrapuntal polyphonic style as a group of men or women gather together to collectively produce the text.[47] Similarly, authority is deferred: 'That's about as far as the story I can give you ... you might be able to get the other half from ... Killer', said a man in Looma as he saw the story he was telling disappear over the horizon into another man's country.

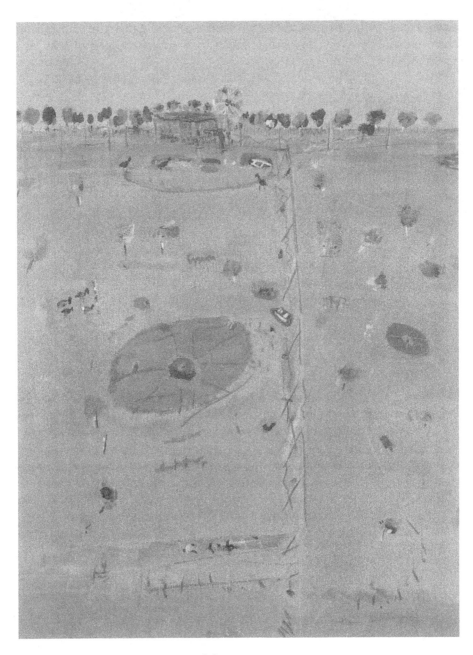

Marmunan

1983, 76.5 cm x 57 cm, gouache and pastel on D'Arches paper.

MAKING RAIN

We call this one *nilababa*[48] -
nilababa belong him -
that's his *nilababa* -
nilababa means his earhole (Laughter) you know?[49] -
yeah *nilababa* -
earhole that's his earhole - -

Me an' my old people used to go before
you know - -
'Ooh poorfella sheep all dead' -
you know? -
too dry country can't get -
dry -
too dry -
sheep can't eat you know - -

'Ooh' my oldfella say, 'Oh' -
'No matter, yunmi go get rain -
look 'round try -
see if we can get some rain for -
make a bit of grass for sheep' -
(Laugh) -
too many dying everywhere -
lil' lil' lambs kicking hungry (Laugh) -
big sheep too - -

So -
he bring me here - - -
all right -
that's my oldman too -
my old father's brother -
young man -

old man died before - -
'All right' he say -
'We must get rain' - - -

So we go in there -
when we go in there - - -
when we go in there - - - -
when we go in there - - - -
before we go to that place weee, gotta chuck all our clothes (Laugh) -
you know? - -
we chuck all our clothes - - -
we must walk there naked -
(Laugh) -
well I, well that's the way he goes you know
Krim: Mm.

'Can we get a mud?' -
we rub ourself with the mud -
you know
Stephen: Red one?
No -
it's the mud from the spring -
finish -

Then we sit down -
then that fella, I sit down -
this fella put his hand inside he get sand -
from inside -
ah must have rain in Broome, er here, *Djarrmanggunan*
we must have-im in *Djarrmanggunan* -
he go in about that deep (Indicates beyond elbow) - - -
rain, er mud - -

Then he sing - -
sing his, I can't sing -
in the tape (Laughter) -
song you know for rain -
all right finish -

'All right you get that spear,' he tell me - -
long spear you know -
proper spear for spearing anything -
then I poke that spear RIGHT DOWN -

right up I go in with the arm too -
'All right pull-im out finish' -
when I pull that spear out -
then I go (Rubs) -
bring everything back make that spear clean (Rubs, laugh) - -

We go back home -
go back for dinner - -
'Er, oh white cloud coming up' (Laughter) -
there, we goin' this way for dinner -
he's over there, mm (Laugh) -
I watchin' too -
'No, watch-im,' he tell me -
he never watch, but I watch-im -
because I must SEE -

So -
stop little bit further -
we look -
hello, gettin' bigger now (Laughter) - -
mmm finish now, he start, gettin' black now (Laugh) -
he come more low too, ready to drop you know -

(Soft) Err we look -
mm -
rain start -
now that big black cloud coming (Laugh) -
rain right through - -
(Soft) he's gone -
just 'round there -
(Soft) finish (Laugh) -
an' we got rain -

We go -
next day I jump on the horse I went loong way too -
'round the fence, no rain -
only we just had that rain in the sheep, paddock -
(Laughter) - - -
this oldfella know how much rain we must get -
(Laugh) -
you know -
so today - - - -

But no lightning -
no lightning no -
no cyclone no lightning nothing -
nothing - -
just the rain - -
good rain -

And that, stone, ice you know what they call that?
Stephen: Hail.
Hailstone.
Stephen: Yeah.
That one -
oh we eat-im too (Laughter).
Krim: Ice-cream.
Ice, like a ice you know little block -
yeah, we suck-em.
Stephen: That's good.
Good eat -

So -
that's it -

Like I said -
If I take somebody stranger - -
You know -
Yunmi pull up there I might tell you break that grass
an' we must take-im -
(Laugh) -
you must take-im - -

All right we off -
we got the grass - -
same thing we see the cloud -
he get bigger an' bigger an' bigger finish -

Then the rain starts -
AND the wind -
oh he break the trees too -
(Laugh) -
AND lightning - - -
and you still got that one -

Might be, I might say 'Oh, finish, chuck 'way! -

chuck-im 'way -
chuck the grass' -
then he finish -

But if you don't chuck that grass he can follow us from sheep station
right up to Broome (Laughter) -
you know -
still come, but if we chuck-im halfway he stop finish.
Stephen: Ah.

We gone now -
wind everything just dead stop -
(Laugh.)

Yeah, well - -
these things we use from *bugarrigarra* -
bugarrigarra bin put the way.

For my   for people you know how to use these things because these
things   have been really somebody walkin' 'round before but they bin
turn into   those sorta things.

But we have stories for them   how we can make these things work
but we never seen nobody   before   (Laugh)   but we must have only
stories you know   how we can make these things work.
Stephen: Yeah.
He must work.

Oh somebody can go there too   I might tell-im story he go there pick-
im-up this one pick-im-up that one he can do what he like he wait and
wait wait wait 'til sundown nothing happening (Laughter)   nothing
happen   'What wrong?   Jees I gotta go in the dark now go back to
Broome'   (Laugh) you know.
Oh he might camp there.
Stephen: Yeah.
He get nothing   but he must know how to, make-im work.

Stephen: Song?
Songs   the way he must act too   you know   he he must oh lots of
ways you know.

That's why we can't teach young people this time   we put lotta things
away from these fellas because   today too much drink in the road   no

91

good for young people they can't use-im, right way.
Krim: Mm.
They use it bad way   good for us we save our, self you know (Laugh)
they can do anything   'cos he's drunk you know   (Laugh) but it won't
work for 'im all the same like I said.

If we only just   teach   just tell-im stories   stories   you know just
tell-im stories   just tell-im stories   if we tell-im stories but they won't
work for 'im   but I mean more, something more bigger you know
we tell-im stories too they only just hear you know   (Gestures 'hard of
hearing', laughter) they can't hear proper you know (Laughter)   yeah.

They like to see it they like to see it, move   but er, sometime they tell
us   'Why don't you people make it move?'   you know   so we can see
'Yes, but er our old people didn't teach us how to move these things
so we can't move-em (Laugh) we can only tell you story'   (Laugh).

See today everybody all want know.
Stephen: Yeah, they want to see.
He want to see.
Krim: 'Facts', yeah.
(Starts rasping)[35]

Rain or cyclone you know   like I said ANYTIME   we can get-im
but we don't want-im   we don't want to   too many families every
-where   you know   we must be good friends.

Well   we know   white people done lotta damage   to the, country
an' we old   we don't worry.

But the old people, what they used to do these things for? because for
reason   they must   they got no tucker those days old people   they
only lived from ground   grass seeds   grass must grow must get his
grass seeds   you know.
Stephen: Yeah.

Er if he want to travel he must have water halfway   all these sorta
things.

Well they got these things for good reason   not for killing people
make it bad you know   but for country.

Just to make you know he can get little, patch of rain here   'nother patch of rain there 'nother little place there in their waterholes   when they go from this place everything all tucker finish oh this grass is growing other side   he's the first one had rain already got seeds (Laugh).

Gwuya-gwuya ni imani dandjina-yana
Mother   she threw herself back

marmunungu larrayi indinj-yana
PLACE   hide away   she said

Mimiyagaman
1983, 76.5 cm x 57 cm, gouache and pastel on D'Arches paper

AT MIMIYAGAMAN

First one must be this one   yeah he there   next one 'nother side
again   we gotta walk from here, eh? you want to see them?
Stephen: Yeah! This is Mimiyagaman?
Mimiyagaman   oh about five or six of them here. (Laugh)   (To
Nangan) *Mimiyagaman.*
Stephen: You starting here eh?
Yeah I think so. (To Nangan) We gotta go bog hole, bog hole, look-im
Djuwarigarra.[51]

(We get out of car.)

Bad one for rain too.
Krim: Butcher Joe's not moving   scared of the bulls I think (Laugh).
Stephen: Mimiyagaman.
Krim: Mimiya
Mimiyagaman   he coming?
Krim: Yep, I dunno about old Butcher Joe.
Oh might be too far for him walk around   he coming?   (Calls) You
coming?   oh, all right.
Krim: Butcher Joe can make the billy, some tea (Laugh).
We shoulda left-im, might cook himself (Laughter).

(Paddy Roe is singing as he approaches the springs.)[52]

This is *Mimiyagaman*   start you know   one spring.

Stephen: It's all right, this water?
Good one, well water all right I think   all spring   spring water all
good   'nother one here never dry   never dry   but we walk in
here very boggy too   that's the middle of it.
Krim: Yeah that little spring in the big spring.
That's where he overflowing from you know.

I don't see any snake here.

Krim: That's a big one isn't it? How many are there, seven?
Two, three   two   about seven I think, altogether   seven or eight.
Krim: Seven or eight.

All springs country   this all my country too.
Stephen: Yeah.
Spirit, you know.
Stephen: All your djila.
Djila   all my *djila*

Krim: Tchaa! This one is full of water!
This one (Laugh)!
Krim: Yeah.

This is a spring too   what that, two three, indit?[53]
Stephen: Three, four, five.
Five   must be two in here   they never dry up.
Krim: Never.
All these springs you know we go there   never dry up   you know
aalways water   never dry up   that's same as *Djarrmanggunan* we
seen you know?   one two three four five here.

Krim: They, they have different names?
Eh?
Krim: Or are they all called Mimiyagaman? *Or are they different —
each one has a name?*
Name, yeah.
Krim: Each one?
Each one   ah! no, it's all *Mimiyagaman.*
Krim: All Mimiyagaman.
No, they got no different name this is all *Mimiyagaman*   one.

That's a little one   that's a little one.
Krim: Down there, yeah.
We come back.
Krim: Okay.
This is the last one.
Krim: There's another one there too.

This is one spring.
Krim: Yeah.
'Nother one.
Krim: Yeah, and that one.
That's the boss.

Krim: That's the boss! (Laughter).
That's the boss, *Mimiyagaman.*
(Everyone speaks at once.)
Krim: It has the grass in it.
Yeah.
Krim: 'Cos it has the grass through.
That's the one I tell you about with the grass.
Krim: Yeah is that the one with (Gesture of stroking beard).
Yeah, that's his this one (Gesture of stroking beard). (Laughter.)
Krim: Yeah the beard yeah.
Ah, this one   this is the boss   *Mimiyagaman*   that grass there that's
his whatname.
Krim: Beard.

Belong to *yungurugu*   snake   *yungurugu* snake   that's his beard
you know   that's him   that's the last one   well he's the boss of the
spring.
Stephen: Yeah.
This one   he's dry there inside.
Krim: Mm (Laughter).
No, he leaking from side   so this is the grass   that's him.
Krim: And this one will stay wet all the time, always water.
Always water, whole lot   whole lot   whole lot.

99

Should be one there too.
Krim: One more.
Yeah one there, yeah that's right, seven   and this is the boss   this is
the boss right?   that's the boss.
Stephen: Yeah, all right.
Mimiyagaman he's the boss   somebody break-im little bit leaves
anything grass and take-im 'way, you know   ooh big rain.
Krim: Is it? No touching.
No touching   rain lightning bad   you know   bad lightning   little
cyclone   always   yeah.

So this is him.
Krim: Yeah.
That's the one I was telling you all the time this is him.

But this one grass used to grow more high but too many cattle and
horses eating it down you know   but it should be very high so
that's him.

Plenty cockle shells too eh?   sea bin here right through   boat used to
sail in this plain   (Laugh) you can see the shells   they never carry-em
from somewhere   (Laughter).

Something floating there   wonder what went   something went inside
might be *barni* or something.
Stephen: Barni I think.
In that water?
Krim: Oh yeah.
Barni barni.
Stephen: You want to get him?
Barni in feeding trough   he all right leave-im   *barni* yeah (Laugh) he

get in trough.
Krim: Big one too.
He in bed now he'll come out in a minute.

Krim: I didn't even see barni *there!*
Yeah *barni* there   so we won't kill-im   he's hungry poor fella.
Stephen: Oh.
He'll get up in a minute   he can't breathe in the water too long   you
know   I can pull-im out for you if you want-im   eh?

He bin makin' hole here   that's his hole (Laugh)   his tucker place

here   this old fella   (Paddy pulls out goanna) not very big one
but he's only a small one   Oh! he's a big one.
Ray: He's a big fella.[54]
Ooh, poor fella skinny one   see-im now?
Stephen: Yeah.
He might bite me too.

(We take photographs.)
That's him?   got him?   all got-im nicely? I'm gonna let-im go eh?
All: Yeah.

Very skinny one (Laugh).
Stephen: He got broken tail too.
Eh?   he got twisty tail.
Ray: He big fella.
Mm big one   I thought was small one   so he have a feed   all right
old man have a sleep   here his hole I think.

Well this is the boss   *Mimiyagaman.*
Krim - Mimiyagaman *yeah.*
But dry time   anybody want water   er rain   anybody want rain
well they get it from little spring   there (Laugh)   shell   cockle.
Krim: Mm.
Few whatname too stone   stone.

101

Stephen: Oh yeah.

Oh yeah he bin messin' around here all the time   that old skinny fella
you know.
Krim: Another barni.
That *barni*, hole belonga him, see?
Stephen: Oh yeah.
He camp in every spring.
Stephen: Yeah.
Well he get feed there, frogs   tadpole you know.
Krim: Mm.
Or big big frogs.
Krim: He must be part of the spring, his home?
(Laugh) Might be his home too, yeah   he dig everywhere.

This is a little one[55]   he's covered with grass.
Krim: Ooh yeah! that's a nice one.
This is his grass   and he's covered with the grass   this one   bad
little   spring   but good too   good too save people   they get water,
rain   good good rain   no, no, no lightning or anything   but good
rain.

Only that one's the bad one, boss man (Laughter)   but this one they
can go in here they can stick spear inside   you know   then they go
(Gesture of throwing clay off the spear)   that white clay they get-im
inside   then white cloud come out straight away   (Laugh) in the open
country   white cloud   they just go under the tree wait for rain to come
(Laugh)   this is him little one.

We can go back through here?
Krim: Yep.
Good.

This is all the spring   this is all my spirit too.
Stephen: Yeah.
You know   anytime I go to sleep I want to come in dream I come here
I never go any other places (Laugh).

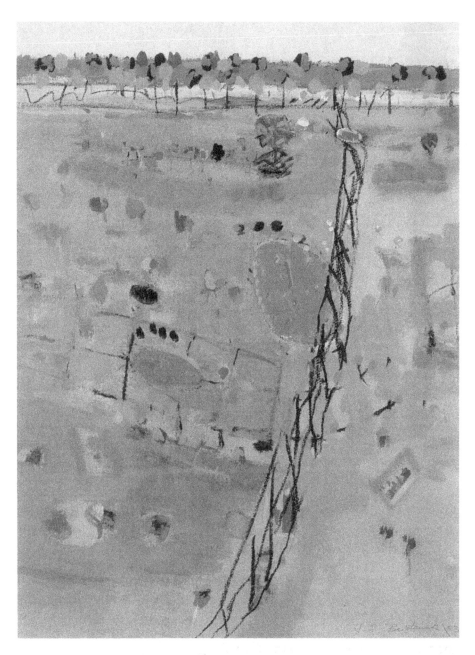

Ilangamugun
1983, 76.5 cm x 57 cm, gouache and pastel on D'Arches paper

DIFFICULTY WITH GREEN (BOREDOM)

Boredom is not far from ecstacy, it is ecstacy viewed from the shores of pleasure.

Roland Barthes.

The quotation from Roland Barthes suggests that boredom has, an intimate relationship with pleasure.[56] In fact, there is no need to see boredom as an unfortunate experience or a waste of time. Each time the reader says that there is no pleasure to be found in one text, he or she is assuming that it will be found elsewhere, in another text about to come into view.

'Boredom' thus labels an extremely important category for any theory of reading. It says that you have read in a certain way, and demands that you take note of *how* you have been reading things (because it is always possible to find a new way of reading a 'boring' text so that there is a sudden rush of pleasure).

For the Aboriginal inhabitant the Plains are a moving text: an eruption of life as a lizard scuttles for safety. Your whole attention is concentrated for a moment, then released in laughter. How can it be that the lizard is both there and not there, and all you are left with is a surprise? And perhaps a flash of memory, a story, because that *djalubardju* (the lizard) is really a little boy, as we shall discover later.

So there is no general sustained level of pleasure or boredom, only 'flashes', only specific meanings for different places or things. Paddy Roe was perhaps 'bored' by the generality of Krim's question, 'Do you feel good about coming back to the Plains?':

Oh yeah good you know   very good.

Only thing country bin change little bit you know   that's why I didn't really feel like to come back to this part of the country.

104

Stephen: You didn't?
Not really you know but I mean er.

I was goin' to get a block of land or something in the station property
you know   little bit in my country but   but I still can't   keep away
altogether from the country because it's my spirit (Laugh).
Stephen: Yeah.
If I don't come like this well I come in dream.
Stephen: Yeah.
I only bin here not long in dream I told old Butcher Joe   you know.
Stephen: Yeah.

So   you know   but I don't tell too many people because it's
mine sometimes you tell too many people nothing come for you.

Old texts from European cultures can become boring and flat as reading
after repetitive reading deposits the same silt of interpretation in the
same places. Some text like Shakespeare's *Hamlet* for instance, starts to
get boring until there is the sudden cyclonic disturbance of a new reading: Freud and psychoanalysis. With this reading the text comes alive
as the words now become the symptoms for the reader's diagnosis of
Hamlet's psychosis or mental illness.[57]

Learning the language of Roebuck Plains is not to discover in it the
same types of features as European landscapes; it is of a different order. There are hills and valleys to be found, but how frustrating for the
European to find that they are so slight; fingers with their sparse covering of gum and wattle stretched out across the mudflats. We have to
see the Plains in terms of a series of tracks and in terms of underground
sources of water. These things are sacred, and around the waterholes
there is permanent green, even at the height of the dry season, when the
Plains might blow with dust.

For the landscape painter the dry Plains present the 'normal' range
of colours—the ochres which have become so familiar in Australian
landscape painting. A green landscape, which is not a forest, presents
a difficulty.

For the nomad, living in the green wet season means living in relative immobility. It is a pause, an interval between the drier seasons
when things get done. For the European migrant in the North, the Wet
is, of course, boring and frustrating—humidity, confinement indoors
or waiting for the rains to 'break'. We took refuge in a friend's work-
shop in town as the rains thundered down and the ceiling fans flopped
around in the humid atmosphere. Krim started work on a series of

paintings which represented our recent trip to the places west of the Old Sheep Camp.

After sketching the outline of the work he cut rounds of paper (the springs) and stuck them loosely on the canvas, then rolled the blue/green paint over the surface which was as flat as the country itself. These rounds of paper were removed from the first painting, modified slightly then transferred to the next one, leaving white spaces which could then be coloured in—sometimes with crayons, imparting a permanent greasiness to the dried acrylics. In Roebuck Plains, the successive groups of springs appear in the 'valleys' between the 'hills' as the track winds westward along the southern border of the Plains Each time a hill is crossed a new horizon appears. With this series of paintings, the variations in the horizons point to these intervals, these successive appearances of new groups of springs and new horizons.

Another theme appearing again in these paintings is that of the boundary fences, the ugly fences which any other painter would be careful not to see (landscape painting is the *artificial* medium which paradoxically reproduces *nature*). Krim cannot ignore them because they are the visible violation of the space he is reading, a reading which is also articulated with Paddy Roe's statements about fences which politely conceal the frustration of his nomadism. Krim's statement is therefore quite a simple one, that these fences are precarious and temporary European impositions on a country which seems not to be made for them. But the disintegrating fence in 'Ilangamugan' (page 103) finally gives away in the following painting 'Gulmugabu' (page 108) to an imaginary function: the protection of the springs. If these springs are to survive, the painting seems to be saying, it will be necessary to enclose them so that the heavy plunging hooves of the cattle don't turn them completely into swamp.

The last painting in the series 'Marmunan' (page 86), carries the most threatening sky and the most formal structure. The furthest point in our journey west, at the place called *Gulmugabu* (and by the Whites, Coolmacop), it is also the most realist and least spiritual statement. It can be compared to the delicate lyricism of 'Mimiyagaman' (page 95). Here we have a large tank collecting water from the windmill, cattle are in evidence, feeding and drinking. The largest spring has undergone a transformation, or it is undergoing a transformation still: from spring to windmill—a metaphor in paint. This is the change in the country mentioned by Paddy Roe, the change which causes him a certain amount of anguish when he comes to look at it and gives the contrast between the visits he can make in his dreams and the ones he actually makes. He also is subject to a certain amount of difficulty when it comes to reading the country: How can he live there now? or rather, how can he imagine himself living there now: 'I was goin' to get a block of land or something'.

This is one of the limits towards which the reading of the country can be pushed: turning it completely over to 'settlement', so that even Paddy Roe can have a dream about a modest 'block of land', a dream which any retirement scheme would want to persuade him to have.

Gulmugabu
1983, 76.5 cm x 57 cm, gouache and pastel on D'Arches paper

SURVIVAL: *DJARLBUNGURU*

Nangan: No waterhole, got big tree   hollow tree.
Yeah.
Nangan: Djarlbunguru
Djarlbunguru, I gotta take you to   I think that's the first thing we're
going to do   might be tomorrow morning   (Nangan laughs) we get-im.
Stephen: Where are we gonna go?
Derby Road   we don't go off the road   we just go on the road and cut
couple o' trees and drop-em on the utility   you know   chuck-em on
bring-em back we'll fix-em up   'cos I want one, them two logs for
Shinju.
Stephen: What do you make? For keeping water?
Waterhole   water in the ground.
Stephen: Oh good.
I'll show you here too you can take a picture of him.
Stephen: I was thinking about that.
Yeah.
Stephen: You told me about that when I was here at Shinju time.
Shinju time   but I cut two this time oh only very light wood   you can
carry one he can carry one   or I can carry one (Laugh).

Waterholes about eight mile apart might be little bit more, in places
might be about eight mile apart.
Stephen: In this country here?
Well in this country now   you know   oh might be only 'bout   four
mile apart   in THIS country   but in the desert is eight mile apart   but
in this country   they only about four mile apart.

But he got, we don't need *djarlbunguru* for this one because there's
lotta er resting water you know?   aah billabongs.
Stephen: You must put them in special place, low place you must put-im?
Yeah, oh I'll show you when we get this one see when we get-im.

See the tree   be about like that (Draws in sand)   the tree is like that
so   the tree is like that   when we dig a hole   we dig hole that way too
more deep   like this one.

An' when we put it in this end we put-im up little bit more high   and
this one here we put-im level with the ground   'cos this is the hollow
part here   an' we put-im level with the ground   but we put-im in a
little ant bed   little flat   anthill?   ant bed you know?
Stephen: Yeah.
Only flat one   we put-im in that one when the rain comes   he fill that
little hole up, this little flat ant bed, water run down here   when he's
full oh he can run away finish   this is full.

All the time.
Stephen: Same as rainwater tank.
Rainwater   all the way two, three   oh three or four between the
waterholes   so people never go too far might be half a mile (Laugh) or
one mile   here water water all the way camp camp camp   they gotta
camp in every   eeer this one   *djarlbunguru*   see this one.

But we can do this one two ways   if we want to fill-im-up there   in
that flat, place we dig hole for him   but 'nother way we can dig a hole
in the er   'nother way again (Draws)   we dig a hole there   for him.

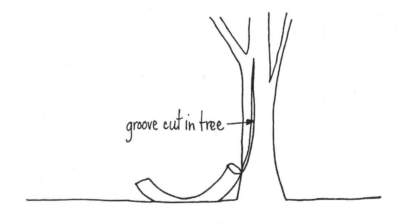

groove cut in tree

An' here's a wattle tree just, tree you know   wattle tree   this one.

I bin tell you about that bark an' things?   we can make boots an'
everything?
Stephen: Boots yeah.
Yeah *mangadj* we call-em[59]   boots   *mangadj.*

Now   from here we cut that, that's the big tree   got branch everywhere   but this one in the ground   so we cut that tree about here   and
take the bark right up to there   an' put-im inside here   so when the
rain come he run down this tree all fill up   he fill this (Laugh) *djarl-*
bunguru (Laugh) you know?
Krim: Good one, yeah.

We cut-im here and take-im back that way little bit an' poke-im inside
here   water run.
Stephen: Oh good.
Oh plenty ways   you can take picture of them too.
Krim: How long it keeps? Long time, the water?
Oh yeah years an' ooh well ants never eat-im too   very hard for ants to
eat 'im   eat that tree.
Nangan: Yeah (Laugh) he last a long time.
Stephen: Yeah, well they left him didn't they?
Yeah.

Oh sometimes three years four years more   sometime they can last
longtime   see lotta dead trees here   white ants never touch-em   they
lay down anywhere you know bulldozer knock-em down.
Nangan: Nobody drink that water, he stand one year twelve months.
Yeah.
Krim: Aah yeah.
'Nother rain come he fill-im up again   but he's full already.

Bird lizard kangaroo anything ooh big drink there too   but they can't
get in inside (Laughter) oh they can if the water go down little bit.
Stephen: Might fall inside.
No no they just walk in that hollow   get a drink and come out again no
worries   nothing never die inside (Laugh)   oh goannas can get inside
but he climb up again   door's open all the time for them (Laughter).

Survival: *Mirdibalang*

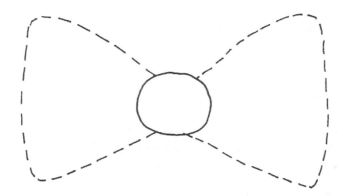

Mirdibalang, we make-im like this (Draws in sand)   only one
little hole there   you know when we dig only one little hole   one
little hole this one   and from there and when we get ooh   might
be about that big I think.
Stephen: To the waist.
Waist, 'nuff   so we can get over   you know climb over.

And then   then rest of the way we dig that way, you see   this kind
inside.
Stephen: Spread out a little bit?
Spread out.
Stephen: How many people?
Ooh three four   three four   no matter he can dig this way too   see?
Stephen: Ah.

Anyway   long as only one door   here   see   one door   and this one
from the bottom   from the bottom, this far from bottom   he about
that
high I think   if any water, rain come in there well he   he   can't run
into the bedroom   (Laugh)   you know   he's like that   he's a
mirdibalang.

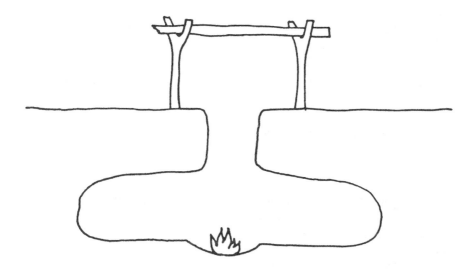

Stephen: And what sort of thing are you using to make-im, digging stick?
Digging stick.
Stephen: Coolamon for carrying that stuff out?
Yeah, with a coolamon   dig-im out with that one   woman job   oh that's their game
Stephen: Oh they're good at digging.
Yeah, but we don't leave much on top   er we gotta leave plenty on top   you know otherways, he fall down.
Stephen: Yeah.
But nothing allasame you can get out of it   (Laugh).
(Ray Keogh arrives, we share our lunch with him.)

Yeah, *mirdibalang.*
Stephen: Mirdibalang.
Mirdibalang, yeah.
Stephen (to Ray): *Cyclone shelters, I just found out about.*
Eh?
Stephen: Cyclone shelters. These people, they don't camp under trees or anything. Cyclone comes, they dig holes, like rabbit warrens.

Yeah, we make hole, and then tunnel.
Ray: Oh.
We sleep everywhere inside   our dog and people and all (Laugh).
Ray: Doesn't fill up with water?
No.
Stephen: Got a water trap at the front.

113

He got.
Stephen: Goes down deeper.
Yeah   yeah.

Well we   we put whatname   in that doorway too   sticks you know
forked sticks   and rail rail rail everywhere an'   this one spinifex, grass
so he don't leak much.
Stephen: How many forked sticks?
Four, an' rail cross very, close together   and then sticks on top of that
One   sticks.

Then we gotta fire in that door oh just a fire but no smoke   we find
good, tree.
Stephen: Which side fire?
In that hole.
Stephen: Underneath the roof
Yeah, underneath the roof   oh roof is long way   he's built, properly
you know so the fire won't get wet   he got fire stick there, one   one
or two 'nuff   pick-em-up from wood, no smoke   he don't smoke
at all.
Stephen: Which one?
Bohemia   and that *banduragu* tree.

We burn aall that one   oh they know, rain time they burn-im whole lot
might be only little bit 'o   here's the wood (Draws)   and this one
might be all burn right up to there somewhere   well they break this one
put the charcoal inside   that big one   but inside he's still burning
you know outside he's, no smoke   but he's already bin burn but he's
burning, all the time and that charcoal can stop right up to the morning
to light 'nother fire again tomorrow (Laugh).
Stephen: Inside the log.
Inside theee, hole   log nothing, we chuck this one away   outside   he
bring too much smoke   might get choke inside you know   only just
quiet charcoal   that's all that's there   but fire always there   no blankets

(Laugh).

Ray: Just charcoal.
Just charcoal.
Stephen: You don't have to wait very long for cyclone to pass.
Eh?
Stephen: Might be passed in, twelve hours, gone.
Something like that.

Stephen: One day.
One day.

Ooh get outside again come back have a sleep   go outside come back
again, sleep (Laugh)   old people you know, too hot, they come out
but 'nuff breeze too   that sand is cold too   wet sand.

Oh plenty ways.

THE EMPTY SPINDLE

One *gardiya* came to the Roebuck Bay area at the turn of the century. Her name was Ada Janet Peggs. The letters she sent back to England describing 'the manners and customs of the native races' were organised by an associate of the Folklore Society into an article.[60]

If a tracker read this piece, he or she would look for signs that told which way Mrs Peggs was heading. A peculiar pressure in her tread might be noticed, something which allowed her to write the way she did at that time (from 1898-1901) and which would not be quite as possible today. This feature in her discourse is her unconscious belief in her *right* to acquire things from the Aboriginal people. A reading of this *discourse of acquisition* might consist in isolating those parts of her text. This will be a selective reading of the text, it leaves out the more patronising traces and the semi-accurate descriptions of Aboriginal societies. It is a reading with a point, since it can indicate the early settlers' ideas about their relations of exchange with the original inhabitants, their economic ideas. It points to their assumed right to take things, while at the same time saying that the blacks only had 'sentimental' value for objects. They 'do not know the value of money':

> The natives here are so primitive that they do not know the value of money, and instead, for a day's work are paid with a stick of tobacco and a pannikin of either flour or rice.

One day a boomerang is given to Mrs Peggs. The gift is accepted (in this account) in a matter-of-fact way which bears no relation to the amount of work which went into it:

> The day before yesterday my husband came to me and took me into the nigger camp to see a man making a kylie; and with the most primitive of tools, scrape, scrape, scraping away, he had been for hours, apparently making no impression on the wood yet very gradually shaping it. Jack saw it in the morning, I in the evening, and then it was far from finished. Next

*day we went again; it was done, and embellished with the dec-
oration of that man's tribe and given to me, 'him good pfeller
boomerang'.*

Mrs Peggs is busily acquiring objects. Even the whites are involved in
the organisation of her obsession:

*On Tuesday, Mr. Macpherson (the Superintendent) gave me
over a dozen black cowrie shells, and Mr. Kenny three glass
spear-heads, which the prisoners in the prison opposite where
we are living had made; one is of white glass, one green, and
one dark smoke-colour. He also gave me a stone tomahawk,
the head most beautifully finished, as smooth as possible, representing an infinite amount of labour; he showed me also
a very fine necklace made of round shells looking like long
bugles, which he says he will divide and give me part of. Old
William, who does an occasional day's work here, had one on
something like it, but this came from a tribe on the other side
of the Bay.*

In the next fragment of her text she describes her acquisitions in an
impersonal language *(I have lately become possessed ...)*. So we wonder
who gave her the firestick. What did they have to trade in order to obtain
it? What return favours might they be expecting from her or her husband?

*I have lately become possessed of a fire-stick which made
the fire for the Kobba-Kobba at last full moon—I believe a
very large one which lasted four days—also a broken kanga-
roo-stick. The one I have is decorated. I asked Billie how it
was done. He said 'all same nail'.*

The value of the objects seems to be related to the difficulty Mrs
Peggs had in obtaining them, the sorts of stories she was told about
them, and their ceremonial importance. These things all relate to their
Aboriginal value. This becomes translated, quite directly, as the value
for Mrs Peggs and the Folklore 'market', as it were:

*Another thing we have; Jack tells me it is of great value, and
cannot imagine how I managed to get it out of the native as
I did. It is a sort of sacred beheading-sword of very heavy
wood, and has seen great service. Jack went to have a wangie
(talk) with the native who gave it, with the weapon, to try
and get him to tell him what the markings meant; but he was
frightened lest some of the other natives should see we had it,
and made Jack hide it under his coat. It appears now it had
been stolen from a camp, and those natives from whence it
came were then out hunting for it.*

117

What powers of persuasion did Mrs Peggs have to use? What sort of risks did the blacks run by handing over sacred/ceremonial objects to whites?

> *The wooden mask of which we have become possessed is not only difficult to obtain but very rarely possessed by a white man. We hear they are not used here, but come from the interior. It is used at the ceremony of man-making. It is placed over the face of the boy after the ceremony is over and for fourteen days he has to wear it, not showing his face to anyone. Every line on the mask is 'talking', telling why the boy is wearing it and so on.*

An important figure at Mrs Peggs' trading post is Ross, a 'King'. He and his wife generously bestow objects on Mrs Peggs. Only *he* can persuade this woman to pay for his goods, and it seems to be a rule she is breaking. 'The natives here are so primitive that they do not know the value of money,' she says above:

> *Ross, the King or Chief of the Roebuck natives, our boy Fred's uncle, is a fine tall man, and speaks English fairly well. On our first introduction to Ross he was wearing twisted by a long hair string round his throat, and then stuck into the side of his hair, a long narrow piece of mother-of-pearl shell; a black end hair twist was fastened on by* wilgy. *Jack wanted it, and after some demur the King gave it to 'Missus' … The next day Ross came again, and brought a splendid hair belt, as well a thick shell necklace which Pollie his wife sent me. Jack told him he wanted a carved shell to 'put along belt' …*
>
> *King Ross sent me a kylie by Mary when she went to his camp. Yesterday at six o'clock a.m. he and Pollie came along. He brought me another kylie, two nulla-nullas, and a walker-berrie, for which he wanted sixpence. I gave it him willingly, although it is the first time I have given money. He also had a drink of tea and a piece of bread and jam. Such small attentions please the natives …*

So there is a variation or two in this general program of acquisition. Sometimes Mrs Peggs gives people bread and jam, tobacco sticks, sixpence. This pleases them, but does the exchange please her? For her the question of pleasure or sociability does not arise because she is collecting and accumulating with 'scientific' and 'objective' rectitude. To talk about her own pleasure of acquisition (which creeps into her discourse nonetheless with adjectives like 'superb' and 'beautiful') would be to display a fetish. 'Such small attentions please the natives …' This unfinished phrase inscribes the social pleasure of an encounter at which gifts were exchanged and food was taken. Yet so much remains unsaid. Perhaps 'King' Ross and Pollie said as they were walking away, 'Such small attentions please Mrs Peggs ...' We have already seen how the labour of the Blacks relates to the objects produced. Other sorts of labour are exchanged at the Peggs' place, and the blacks have to assure them a constant supply. According to Mrs Peggs the people are grateful for the work:

Just lately our boy Kelly prepared for and went on his month's holiday. He had provided a substitute, who, however, did not turn up ...

On Saturday William came up to me at dusk mysteriously, and took from his head a tuft of feathers attached to a bone, which he presented to me. I asked what it was, and he said, 'Feathers along of kangaroo bone'. He told Jack when I was not there that the bone was a human one, taken from the arm of a man killed. It is gruesome to me; however it is not a thing many possess. The feathers are cockatoo. David gave Jack a kangaroo-bone the day he took William to work for us; in gratitude, as William is David's brother ...

Monday I came across William very busy (when he should have been carrying water for the house) with a bit of glass and a nail; also a piece of stone laid on the sole of his foot, on which the nail was being sharpened, and occasionally the glass rubbed. I asked what it was. The answer, 'Spear-head'. It is now ours. The only other acquisition we have made is a 'Yandie', the native cradle or basket made out of a piece of bark, I am hoping to get one made of wood, but the women will not readily part with them ...

This last text points to the difficulties Mrs Peggs had sometimes in her acquisitions. The only thing that stops the women from handing over their *yandi* or *coolamons* is, according to the narrator, 'sentiment'. Again, she has not thought of the immense amount of labour which must go into the production of one of these objects:

The bark pingins of yandi are easily procurable, but those hewn out of wood are not so. I have had two of the latter in my hands, almost thinking them mine; but no! at the last minute sentiment stepped in and I could not get them. The bark pingins are made from the bark of the tree which Mary tells me is called Mourrya; another name is the tea-tree or paper-bark ...

One day 'Mary' came in from the bush and had her hair cut to make a hair belt, or hair string. She obtains a hat, for which the purpose is

119

quite obvious, by baldly announcing 'Me wontum yat'. She received an old bush hat because Mrs Peggs 'had not one to spare'. As Mary is spinning the hair, Mrs Peggs tries to relieve her of the labour of her hands, with no success. No doubt it was destined for someone else.

In turns we greeted her, and then, 'Missus, bring 'em along scissors, I want cut 'um Mary's hair', and the poor creature was shorn of all her flowing locks; after which 'Me wontum yat'. I had not one to spare, so Jack gave her his old hard felt hat. Yesterday morning she set Magdalene, who is her daughter, to wash up; and I, going round to the kitchen by the back door, saw her busily weaving her locks into a belt. I was interested in watching her, and tried all my powers of persuasion to induce her to give me the hair twisted on the spindle; but no, she would not. She, however, gave me the empty spindle.

Mrs Peggs ends up with the empty spindle. She goes inside and adds it to her collection, a collection which became a photograph in an old British folklore journal, with all the pieces numbered. Ada Janet Peggs then opens her diary and makes her ethnographic entries, spinning out her poor words about the things she has acquired; the threads of experience gathering and forming on the empty spindle.

Like Mrs Peggs, we are all spinners of texts. In retrospect we can unravel her fabric and point to its absurd designs, so out-of-date and inadequate to the needs of 1984. But is this text any better? It has appropriated Mrs Peggs' text and woven it into its own design in the same way she appropriated the artifacts; an assumed right to criticise and quote. It must be remembered that her text was not just the inscription of colonial experience, it was seen then as a writing which was an enlightened approach to that experience, an alternative to some more blunt and racist ways of constructing it. The conditions for enlightenment still exist; whenever we go to pick up the spindle it is empty.

'WE BETTER GO BACK TO COUNTRY'

One night we were playing with the goat at Coconut Wells.

And this one is Pepinu (Laugh).
Stephen: You've got a name for that —little one —my child coming up?
Oh we'll have to call him name.
Stephen: Mighta been some rai *around here you know.*
Might be *rai* from here   yeah.
Stephen: I don't know if they would come to white women.
Weell   no might be eh?, never know   might be *rai* from here too.
Stephen: Might be.
Or might be YOU, you know (Laugh).
Stephen: I must have something to do with it.
Yeah (Laughter) well I mean.
Stephen: Well that's my work.
Yeah   well just like me when my daughter   Teresa.[61]

Yeah I -
me an' my old woman was working for -
for a bloke called Douglas, Mr and Mrs Douglas -
oh one old white fella - - - -

So - -
I gave him a hand -
he had some pigs and all that -
pigs, an' growing ginger -
this is in *Minari* you know?
Stephen: Minari
Minari, Minarinj we call-im -

Minarinj better I think - - - - - - -
(Soft) yeah - - - - - -

So we worked there - - -
so that was Sunday one morning I said to my old, lady I said old woman
   you know I said er, 'I think yunmi better go down the beach today' -
'Yes, all right,' he say -
try to get some stingray - -
we wanted to have something fresh you know -
we had salt meat all the time -
(Laugh) dry salt meat -

So we went down the beach - -
old woman said, 'I'll wait here for you' -
so he wait in the shore outside you know in dry place -
I went down -
the tide was coming in too -
I meet the tide when the tide was coming in I stand up there -
see I gotta stand up then I can see the fish then they come you know
   anyway - -

So I seen this black thing coming up -
first - - -
oh I said might be shark ooor might be seaweed something -
I didn't take much notice -
so I looked around -
see if I can see fish, lotta fish was, passing to -
I throw spear but I couldn't get anything -
too fast - -

So I looked again -
oh he's coming very close -
oh I better see what this thing coming I said -
it was coming, straight for me (Laugh) -
when I looked, oh (Breathy voice) stingray -
you know his flappers going like this (Gestures) -
(Growl) ooh stop quiet now he's coming -
I hardly know, hard to see I just watch him, I was standing up -
put me spear down -
coming coming he come straiiight for me I thought he gonna turn
   somewhere so I can get behind him and follow him from behind -
but he come straight for me, straight, right up to my leg -
riight up, when he got up close, stand up (Laugh) -

123

right up -
just stand up -
then I got the spear -
toop, I got-im right in his flappers -
you know -
if he wanted to pull away oh he can get out -
just in the flappers (Laugh) -
no (Chuckle) he didn't want to get away -
So I got-im -
I picked him up with the spear I took him right up to the beach -
quiet! -
when I chucked him outside an' he start to (Laugh) dance around a bit
     you know (Laughs) -
(Soft) ah, that's all -

I cut his, thorn off his tail -
pull him right up to, where old woman was sitting down -
we made a big fire an' have a good feed oooh fat! (Laugh) -
fat -
for this one we cut one, one side, we eat all that one side -
and fat one side fat -
they got big fat you know -
and the other fat and the one side[62] -
I took that back for my boss -
(Laugh) Mr and Mrs Douglas -
oh they eat anything too -

So they made a biig curry for us -
(Laugh) with that one -
mm -

(Soft) All right I said to him -
so -
we had curry for supper -
outa that one (Laugh) but we eat the other one already fresh -
(Soft) all right -

Ooh, we bin there 'bout - - - -
six seven weeks eight weeks just on two months anyway -
in that place working 'round -
and eeeer - - -
well my old woman really you know said to me er, 'I think we better go
     back to country -

we got no people here you know' -
'Yeah that's right,' I said -
'You feel like to go back?' -
'Yes' she said -
'Oh me too,' I tell-im, 'I like to go back too' -

But I -
I go back for some reason too -
you know I had that in my mind -
what this eeer, well I, I wanted to go back too -
to get clear with these people[63] -
you know, more quick -

So all right, I work -
next morning aall day -
in the garden -
feed the pigs -
work in the garden -
ooh just -
messin' around you know - - - -
'til about tea-time, supper time -
we had our supper an' everything -
we made a fire in the camp -
you know we sleep 'longside the fire -
me an' the oldwoman - -
that was south-east time too, cold time
cold, cold time - -
(Soft) aah -

Soon as he got little bit dark -
so nobody can see us we roll up all our swag an' everything I chuck the
    swag on me shoulder -
picked up the other little girl -
you know (Laugh) pick 'im up -
well his oldwoman could carry him -
from the hill you know we went down the beach -
and put-im down again in beach then -
(Laugh) -

So we went down the beach an' we off - - -
aall the way, footwalk -
oh we musta walk 'bout -
oh nearly, nearly four miles I think, you know -

'Oh I think we better sleep,' old woman got tired you know -
said to me we better sleep here somewhere, 'Yeah yeah,' I feel tired too
    oh big weight I was -
oh big weight I was carrying too you know tucker swag water -
water old woman got the kerosene tin in his head (Laugh) -
that's right! -
mm, kerosene tin of water -
you know them square tins, kerosene tins?
Stephen: Mm
Mm -

(Breathy) All right, so he put -
I grabbed the drum, tin off his head -
put-im down -
put the swag out, laid the swag out -
all right we aall sleep now -
we had the little girl in the middle -
old woman was other side, me this side -

Aah I shut me eyes now old woman get up -
you know he can hear something -
(Breathy) 'Hey, hey,' said, 'Get up' -
(Breathy) 'What there?' -
(Breathy) 'That boss and missus they must be here somewhere, they're
    looking, can hear 'em whistling,' said -
(Breathy) 'Somebody here, on top,' she says -
(Breathy) 'Ooh yeah might be too, they mighta track us up,' I tell-im -

I get up -
'Oh yeah, that's right' -
like a whistling, but it's more like a crying (Laugh) you know eer little
    baby crying veery you know -
(Soft) 'Ah' -
(Breathy) 'Oh yeah must be' -

So we roll our swag and off again -
old woman put that kerosene tin on top his head, OFF again -
went right up -
oh might be about mile I think -
we get tired you know half sleepy too -
(Breathy) 'I think this'll be all right,' say -
'We sleep here' -
we sleep right in the cliff you know, big high cliff there, but right inside -

126

inside -
where this man can't jump down too -
(Laugh) or somebody -

All right - -
unroll all our swag -
oh we didn't unroll the swag but we just wait little while -
no, no noise -
so unroll the swag now -
put-im out bed everything we got sleep now, nice sleep (Fade away)

Child: (Interrupts) Lulu,[64] *got two dollar?*
I haven't got it   you better give 'im a punch, I dunno no I haven't got
any   money   no   (Sigh) nothing   you better tell-em nothing.
Child: Yep.
No small one, Baba   no   tell-em to have a rest little bit.

'All right,' I said to -
ah, I went to sleep again 'cos I bin workin' you know I get tired more
    quick -
so I went off to sleep and this old woman hear the same noise again -
whistling -
(Soft) whistling -

I get up, he wake me up again, 'Hup, hey!' -
(Breathy) 'That must be them people looking for us, for track you know' -
'Ooh yes yes right listen,' I get up -
I listen again SAME thing again SAME thing again somebody coming
    crying just like you know ooh like a whistling but throat very you
    know like whistling like a baby crying[65] -
we never think about that thing too you know (Laugh) - -

So we roll our swag again -
off we went -
this time we went oh -
little bit more long way now - -

So when we went up to that -
we find a place again good place stony place you know -
stony place we find we go inside there now we stop inside that place -
unroll our swag again - -
you know - - - - - -

127

Unroll our swag -
Ah, an' he look -
(Soft) 'You see anything?' -
we listen -
I never go to sleep this time -
I was 'wake now -
old woman go to sleep first -

So we went to sleeep I couldn't hear nothing -
so they musta give old woman good chance to sleep might be (Laugh)
    you know, something -
'All right,' I said, no matter - - -
we get up next morning, nothing trouble us -
we climb up, we went right up to Price Point -
Price Point, oh not very from Price Point we camped too -
oh we didn't know - -
we didn't know the country anyway -

So when we get up there we off -
I climb up, 'Oh motor car road,' I said -
'We better follow this motor car road' -
so we followed the road now aall the way
right up -

When we got half way -
when we got half way -
we just went through the tree you know -
'Oh might be good tree this lot' -
I know the trees too you know, for honey -
'I better have a look at one of these tree' -
when I went around have a look at that tree oh I seen wild honey you
    know his thing, nest -
'Ah we got honey here,' I said -
ah *waladja waladja*, we say -
honey we call him *waladja* -
'You better sit down old woman,' I tell-im -
I'll chop this tree -
I chopped that tree up - - - - - - - - - -

Yes I cut that tree -
'Aah, all right,' I said -
'Better give me that billycan I'll put all that honey in the billycan you
    know' -

well that billycan was full - -
one billycan -
oh, something like a milktin size you know -
this big milktin?
they're only paint tins they used to use for boats (Laugh) -
those days -

So all right -
I put stick down, 'Oh too much,' I said, 'I have to cut him again' -
so I cut 'im again -
we fill another billycan up again -
that's two billycan that's all the billycan we had our tea billy -
fill the two billycan up -
I put the stick down again that tree -
oh still, honey going down -
'Ah, so what we gonna do with this one we gonna leave-im?' -
'No, we cut-im,' old woman said to me -
'Ah, all right then,' I said -
'What we gonta put-im in?' -
'Oh, cut some, white gum' -
gurdinj we call-im you know, bark[66] -
so I got nice one like a boat -
big one too -

So I cut-im again -
it's near the bottom now -
we fill that little dish up oh right full again -
finish -

All right -
I put the stick down again oh he still goin' down! -
'Oh yeah,' so I dig little bit, I cut little bit more -
an' I got little bit more outa that one, put-im in that same, dish you know
    bark dish -
I put the stick down again oh still 'Oh no no,' he say, 'Leave-im, might
    be devil' (Laugh) -
'Oh, all right,' I say -
so we leave the rest, we're off -

But that's only eeer was given to us by somebody, *rai, rai* -
you know mm *rai* -
so we're gone -
we just pick up our swag and honey and everything oooh -

big load again with the honey and everything -
more weight we had to carry -

Aah we just hear *ting ting ting ting tring tring tring* you know -
(Breathy) 'Hello,' I say, 'Somebody coming' -
I look, 'Oh, windmill' (Laugh) you know goin' 'round -
fan, 'Ooh,' we right, we got water -
we only had little bit water left in the kerosene tin too (Laugh) -
so we're off -
we come up, we sit down -
old woman wait for me outside I went there and get some water, cold
    water you know from windmill -
and then two old woman come out in me -

'Oh' -
'Hello'
'Hello,' we say -
'Where you come from?' -
Oh I come from *Minari,*' I tell them, 'From *Minarinj*' -
'Oh -
oh' -
'But proper I come from Roebuck Plain,' I tell em -
'Me an' this old woman we come from Roebuck Plain' -
'From Roebuck Plain?'
'Yes' -
'Ah, -
'From station -
(Soft) from station' -
(Soft) 'Ah -
yupella long way from country -
what yupella doing up this country in 'nother people country?' you know
    strange country -
'You bin here before?' -
'No,' I tell em, 'I dunno nothing -
we only bin come up with boss and missus belong to us you know -
they bring us up here' -
(Soft) 'Ah' -
'you must be *Nyigina* man,' they tell me -
'Yes!' I tell them,
'Ohho, good! we *Djaberdjaber* people' -
they talk to me in *Djaberdjaber,* ooh can't stop -
then they talk to me in *Nyigina,* that two old women -
they can talk *Nyigina* too -

130

Aah well we was all right -
'Come on yutupella must be hungry,' they tell us -
'We got plenty, damper plenty fresh meat,' they get meat from station
    that's their ration -
rib bone cooking in the fire, ooh nice -

So they took us there and we give them aall that, billycan of whatname,
    two billycan honey, one each (Laugh) -
biig feed -

All right - - - - - - - - - -
'All right,' he said -
'We gotta week this one to move we gotta go to Barred Creek,' they tell
us -
'See some more people there' -
'Ah yes,' we said -
'So yupella better come with us too, nobody will be here, you know,
    they said -
'All right,' we say -

So we just gettin' ready to go you know oh we started off 'bout -
from here to the building -
old woman, my old woman get sick -
'Oh,' he tell me, 'I get sick little bit' -
(Soft) 'Oh, what wrong?' I say -
'I dunno,' he say, 'must be that honey, *waladja*' -

'All right,' I tell this two old women, 'Oh this old woman mine gettin'
    sick, we better stop here' -
'Oh well we all better go back to camp,' say, so we all come back to
    camp we camp there, 'til next morning -
next morning my old woman was all right -

We off again -
we had dinner halfway -
in Quondong -
there's a windmill there too -
slow walk -

So we went, in the afternoon we got to Barred Creek -
ooh plenty people there - -
old people -
that's only far as these two old women go, to Barred Creek -

131

All right we camped there that night -
next morning I said to these old people, 'I gotta go back now' -
oh they was very sorry too you know they want us to stop there but I
    tell-em no -
we feel like to go back to country you know -
we feel little bit out of place (Laugh) -
'All right,' they said -

We off - - - -
'Just follow the motor car road,' you know, they tell us where the station
    is too, call in the station -
some of my people there too, you know -
three - - -
two people I think, two -
(Soft) that's all right, we come there -

So when we got up halfway we can hear the motor car coming -
he come from Barred Creek side too -
behind -
'Hello!'
that's the boss, old Denham -
station boss -
Mr and Mrs Denham -
more other people too -

When they come -
'Ah,' he ask me 'Ah, Gooday,' he said -
'Where you from?' -
I tell-im from Roebuck -
Roebuck Plain, station -
he ask me same thing, what I do and I say, 'I bin -
run away with this woman I steal this woman from somebody you know
    (Laughter) -
'Ah, oh yeah might be big fight eh?' -
'Yes, oh yes,' I tell-im -
'Oh must be I tell-im big fight all right -
waiting for me' -
'An' what you gonta do?' -
'Oh well, I might camp halfway and then I push on to Broome,' you
    know -
'All right,' he said, 'Chuck all your swag on the motor car' -

I chuck all me swag on top, you know, on the rack -
put everything on -

and little girl they had enough little room for -
girl -
they couldn't put us on -
was no room -
so we walked -
right up, to station - - - -
supper there too waitin' for us all ready -
so they gave us supper -
(Soft) everything -

And now finish supper boss come out he said to me -
'Ah, we got branding on -
tomorrow morning,' he said er, 'We start branding' -
'Ah yes,' I said -
'So you like to give us a hand for little while,' he said -
'Well er, I didn't think about that way,' I said (Laugh) -
I was gonna go straight back, you know back - - -
Broome or stay at Roebuck Plains - -
'Oh,' he said, 'Never mind you can come back after' -
'I'll bring you after branding' -
'All right,' I said -
I was happy I had some people there too -
some people

So we stop there now   now I was there from that time 'til today
(Laugh)   never go back to my country   you know   Roebuck Plain
oh I go back all right you know sometime but   but I mean to live there
you know   that's the finish, I find out this country was good now this
side   better than my country (Laugh)   oh   not, well people good too
old people   only old people there   but them old people that's the old
people, old *Djaberdjaber* people.
Stephen: The old Djaberdjaber, *yeah.*
Yeah that's the people I showed you in the, paper inside there?   That's
the people I come to   oh about sixty seventy people was there you
know   only old people, they got no children.

Stephen: You stopped there for a long time?
I eer was there well I came there what nineteen   nineteen thirty-
three my, two daughters born   nineteen thirty-three one, nineteen
thirtee-four 'nother one (Laugh)   mm   two   ah, I musta come there
well I was   there for   nineteen, I said nineteen thirty-four? and
thirty-three   well I was there one year before my two little, no   this is
in the same year, nineteen thirty-three when I come up   that was

early   you know beginning of the   that south-east month   you know cold weather?
Stephen: Mm.
Eeer what's this month?
Stephen: May.
May, yeah, beginning of May I musta got there because   that's the time they start   branding   you know in the stations.
Stephen: Yeah.
They only just start   well from that time to this time I never, leave the country   you know.

When my -
first daughter born -
first daughter born -
an' he was a little one -
he born in the bush, in station, no hospital -

So when he born -
my old woman took notice you know -
he musta think about that -
you know the stingray I killed?
in that place -
come up, straight up and stand up in my leg -
and the girl got mark you know he had a look -
got hole in there -
in the hand
Stephen: Mm.
One side arm, right place too, oh this side I think - - - - - -

Well I couldn't get near my old woman you know he had his[67] -
when he had the baby -
when the baby born -

So he sent, 'nother woman -
'You tell that man (Laugh) about the stingray,' he tell-im -
he bin spear-im in *Minarinj* -
this girl now he got hole in his arm (Laugh) -
that's the *rai* - -
that's the *rai* -
Stephen: Mm.

Oh! before that -
we had a -

134

that old woman I said to you he's a doctor too -
Maban -
woman
Stephen: In the windmill?
No, in that station -
well he told my old woman -
he told my old woman -
he say, 'You got my two *rai?*' -
'Where from?' he tell-im -
From *Minarinj*
you bin pick-em up, two girl,' he tell-im -
two girl

(Child interrupts.)
This is one of 'em.
Stephen: Yeah. (Laughter.) *First one?*
No, second.
Child: Two dollar.
I haven't got any money, Baba   I only got twenty dollars.
(We dig out some silver.)
This one last one, 'nother one, Teresa.

All right -
'You got my two *rai*,' he say -
'Oh, I don't know,' he tell-im, my old woman tell-im -
oh he know too but -
old woman didn't know -
but that's the -
that's the country woman that old fella old woman now, he from
    Minarinj - -
that's his country, aall that there *djarngunbar* people you know all
    djarngunbar -
behind from *Minarinj* right through that way you know riight up to
    Beagle Bay road riiight past Beagle Bay road that's their run -
that bit -
that's the old woman tell-im, 'You got two girl,' he tell-im, 'Mine, *rai* -
I see them but they won't come to me -
you've got them two there -
come to you all the time' -
(Breathy) 'Yes?' he tell-im -
'Yeah' -
'I don't know,' he tell-im -
'I KNOW, they're mine, that's my two *rai* (Laugh) -
you're gonna have two baby -

135

that's all the baby you're gonna have -
only that two -
no more after that one,' he tell-im -
'How you know?' he tell-im -
'I KNOW,' he tell-im -
he doctor woman that fella two, *maban* -
we call-em *djanggungurr* -
(Soft) mm, yeah -
'Aah' -

All right that was true first one born, with that mark (Laugh) in his
hand -
this one born again -
next one -
after that one nomore -
(Laugh) no baby -
that's all only two girl -

That's all I had -
my own, other one's -
I got two altogether but other one I picked-im-up a baby -
'nother one -
he belong to 'nother father[68] -
you know -

All right he say -
'Oh well, that's all right,' he said, 'Never mind' -
so we had, two girl, born then -
they belong to that country now *Minarinj* -
Minarinj country belong to them people, *rai* - -
(Soft) mm -

Oh old woman only die not very long too, that old *maban*, woman you
know –
belongs to these two *rai* -
oh, good while back I s'pose - -
might be 'bout - -
seven, eight years ago, not very long -

So -
that's the finish -
so we work in that station -
Christmas-time come -

oh boss ask me now, 'I gotta run these people to Barred Creek, for their
  holidays, and some to Willies Creek, for their holiday and where you
  gonta go? You goin' with these people too?' 'No,' I said, 'I gotta go
  to Broome -
Broome -
I gotta go to Broome I gotta - -
I gotta make all these people -
square' -
you know 'cos I -
pinched his woman from somebody -
so I gotta make all this fellas I gotta make them clear -
come out in them you know -
'Oh, good' -

So he run me to - -
town that time to Broome here -

When he run me here an' -
few other people too belong to that country they follow me -
some walked -
from station right up to Broome - -
so all these fellas er -
I come out for these fellas first week -
I come out, in Broome, big fighting ground just here now in this -
in this land here we got you know we got the other land other side here -
this one -
that's a big fighting ground -
biig open place you know -
fighting ground - -
good -
Anne Street? Anne Street reserve?
Stephen: Yeah.
Yeah but not, that one, it's more like this side -
the road went straight a -
cross
Stephen: Mm
And the fighting ground was each side of that one -
(Laugh) -
(Soft) mm -

So I come out for these fellas -
biig fight -
this right man come first -

you know ooh -
oooh shoulda seen him coming you know ooh -
(Creaky voice) we had a fight fight fight fight fight fight fight you know -
we fight with sticks -
karli, karli first, *karli* fight -
finish -

Ooh few hits with the stick then -
but too many women there too you know they stop us they stop these
    people well they stop me too stop these fella -
so old fella's on the losing side you know he's finished he's falling
    down (Laugh) -
ah so, cut-im-out you know no more fight finish -
(Soft) ah -

(Soft) All right -
old fella stop too -
I stop too -
go back -
aaall this mob now I come out again -
me and the old woman come out again -
I come out in this old fella I put the spear for him you know I 'Stand-im
up here,' I say; 'Here the spear' I give him my leg to 'im you know[69] -
I stand up -
put my leg out -
I stand up for him, nothing in my hand (Laugh) -
(Soft) so -

Well that's the way they, make everything clear you know, in the fight -
you must put spear through me no matter five six time all the same -
he knock me down all the same -
you know I fall down -
(Laugh) - -

He watch that spear - -
'No,' he say -
he pull that spear out, chuck-im in the ground (Laugh) -
he come up to me he grab me this kine he go this way you know (Shows
    embrace) -
'That woman is yours -
(Laugh) and the little fella too' -
the girl belong to him -
'That's yours' -

no bad friend nothing -
he just leave-im be -

So old woman come around too he had *milgin* -
milgin we call that's er -
digging stick
Stephen: Digging stick yeah
Big one you know -
he stand-im-up too, for all the womans you know -
he comin' everyone, all the woman come -
now all the women come 'nother one come front boss woman he pull
    that *milgin* chuck-im down in the ground -
no more -
'You follow-im *yargu* belonga you' (Laugh) mm -
can't hit us no more finish -

So they -
just like we bin get married too you know -
full –
that's in the tribal, way -
you see -
we get married that way, church too you know they get married, some,
    but we get married that way -
that's tribal wife -
this is the way now -
(Soft) mm, finish -

'You tupella got little girl -
that's your man' -
(Soft) mm -
so here we are (Laugh) oh the old woman's gone anyway -
I lost 'im -
(Soft) you know -
well that's the way - - - -
(Soft) mm -
well this is the way you know

But this is the way I feel too you know ah   there's plenty woman I can
    see here but nothing for me you know you know I lost my, old woman
    so I sooner live without a woman.
Stephen: Like my dad.
Eh? Yeah.

139

Stephen: Same.
Same, eh.
Stephen: Mm.
Yeah I see plenty woman walkin"round it's not inside of me (Laugh) I
    lost one, finish, gone   (Soft) mm.

I show you the photo, this old woman too.
Stephen: Oh yeah.
With the children (Laugh) you know   with all his grandchildrens.
Stephen: Is it all right for you to be without a woman?
I dunno, but I feel more happy   without a woman (Laugh)   see?
Stephen: Mm.
(Soft)Mm   well, I stand up straight, you know, strong   because, I
don't worry for nobody   oh I talk to people, it's all right but   but ah
that's all right   but I feel more happy too   (Soft) you know   I dunno
what keep me happy but   I'm always, the same (Laugh) you know   I'm
not worrying I should help that fella or I should take that fella, you
know I er   somebody talk to me and I look from long way, 'Yairs?'
(Indicates a look of detachment. Laughter.)   (Soft) mm.

(Recommences story with gusto.)
All right that was finish now the last bloke come that's the son now
    belongs to my old woman -
big boy, man he was -
only young fella too -

So I come out for 'im -
last one -
that fella, but that was sundown, rain time now that's Christmas time,
    you know -
Christmas time, lotta grass you know these long spear grass come up -
he dark
Stephen: Her brother?
No, my old woman's son -
he had 'nother son
Stephen: Grown up man?
Yeah man grown up man, only young man too -
two two - - -
he had two sons -
he had two sons -
that was one of the sons, oldest son, other one was still little boy yet, you
    know, in the bush, oh big man - - - -

140

All right, so this fella I come out for 'im and he throw boomerang, now
    he was left-hand too you know -
when he throw that boomerang -
I couldn't see, it went in the grass you know -
and I, I can only feel something touch me like this (Brushes trousers) -
but that *karli* stick in my, leg -
see-im here (Rolls trouser leg) - - - -
(Laugh)
Stephen: Mm
See-im there?
mm that's the stitches -
doctor put in you know -
that's the boomerang mark -

So when I come up -
when I come up -
when I went back to these people now somebody tell me 'Oh you got
    blood running down your leg' -
'Oh, oh might be that thing only bin just (Brushes trouser leg) pass,' you
    know I say -
might be -

When they feel-im, roll my trousers up -
I had long trousers -
and they roll-im-up they find this, *karli,* 'Oh you got *karli* sticking in
    you -
karli sticking in you,' they tell me -
(Breathy) 'Aah' -
somebody pull-im-out *pheeew* you shoulda seen the blood like a pipe
    water (Laugh) -
I just fall down when the blood left me you know come down like a dead
bullock (Laugh) BANG -
(Soft) mm, all right -

One old fella, three man anyway witchdoctors they come up - -
they want to stop this blood you know -
they put, something -
they had them witchdoctors -
you know they finish blood stop -
dead stop once -

And then that oldfella went back and got the wheelbarrow for me they

    put me on the wheelbarrow -
took me up to hospital, in wheelbarrow -
no motor cars
Stephen: What did they put, these fellas?
Ah smoke -
that's all they put feathers, feathers you know -
eaglehawk feather -
finish dead stop then I went to hospital

(Soft) That's all   so we leave-im for a while that's the finish.

How Shall We Write History?

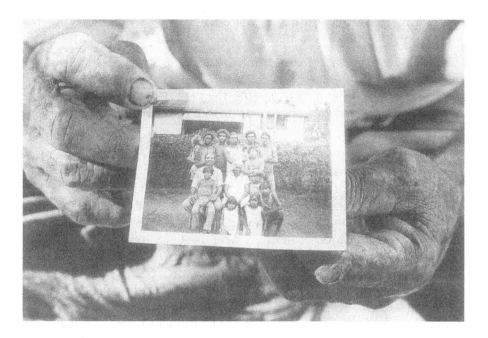

The misfortune of history is the responsibility it is forced to bear, the responsibility of telling us what happened in the past so that our present and future actions will be guided with this knowledge. And it has been the Left which has asked so much of history, insisting that it go beyond the orthodox demand for a history which maintains a continuity with the values of the present, a history which would never contradict current conceptions of 'common-sense'. The most 'obvious' history to write is the one which celebrates the achievements of the powerful, using the language of the powerful. When the Broome Shire Council sought a writer to depict the town's last hundred years, they went to Hugh Edwards, the 'right man for the definitive book on Broome', as one reviewer put it. This same review emphasised the pearling industry and didn't use the word 'Aborigine' once.[70]

These are the gaps in histories that cause questions to be asked, questions coming from people other than the rich and powerful, people whose poverty and powerlessness in fact made it possible for the first to live their easy lives. Successive rewritings of history would then become a task of producing different sets of stories about ordinary people, about Aborigines, about women; not in the name of the 'truth', as if the ruling class historians were distorting facts for their own ends, but with the idea of seeing history as always being written within political formations.

How then does one proceed to write? The latest challenge to historical orthodoxy has been to discuss the shape of the text of history. This is how this challenge was put by the Aboriginal working party for the Bicentennial History Project:

> *When the cues, the repetitions, the language, the distinctively Aboriginal evocations of our experience are removed from the recitals of our people, the truth is lost for us. The form and structure will not be passed on to others and they are denied the right to look after the heritage and in turn to pass it on.*[71]

What figures does one emphasise in writing history? The individual or the class? Ordinary people or 'great' people? Does one talk about them or does one let them speak for themselves? Can they be interrupted? How is history organised around concepts of time? Is time linear and regular, as in dates, or does it repeat its structures?

It is only recently that the chronology of Australian history has been pushed back beyond 1788. Since, say, 1972, that great turning point in Aboriginal politics when the tent embassy put Aboriginal Affairs high on the agenda of the Whitlam Government, Aboriginal people have demanded a place in the chronicle of Australian history, or rather they demanded recognition of their prior sovereignty over the lands of the continent. That voice, endlessly repeating, 'We were here before you', finally reached the ears of the historians and they started to gather material from the archives. History is thus programmed according to the needs of the times.

Within the issue of Aboriginal sovereignty there is more at stake than the use of lands; there is the right to control the production of Australia's mythologies. Most importantly there is our conception of 'nationhood', and it appears that Aboriginality is the commodity which is being bargained for in exchange for Aboriginal land and institutional power and control. 'Tell us what you are really like,' say the white institutions, 'Dance for us once more and sing your songs. We will say to the world that this too is our *Australian* heritage: this is the nation which can stand proud amongst others because it has a timeless history in the Aboriginal peoples.'

As long as Aboriginal cultures have the role of representing timelessness then the story of their more recent history will tend to be put to one side, or that too will be brought forward as more evidence of the continual struggle of an eternally oppressed people; always the same as they were from the beginning. A more specific history would have to account for reversals in trends, for victories as well as repetitious failures. And when these so-called victories are looked at afresh, can they be celebrated once again, or does the weight of oppression reduce them also to the state of affairs we are so used to hearing about? The strategic importance of history is lost if it is allowed to become the 'same old story'.

Aboriginal History, a new sub-branch of academic history, has uncovered a new domain and a new positivity. Its domain is made up of two sets of materials; archives relating to Aboriginal people, and these people's spoken history. The positivity is created with phrases like Aboriginal 'point of view' - a metaphor also at work in the title of the book, *The Other Side of the Frontier*.[72] The positive statement is that 'our' history is now going to be seen, for the first time, through Aboriginal eyes, and that 'they' opposed 'us'; there *really was* Aboriginal resistance to invasion and the history which represented the Aborigines as peacefully giving way to superior strength was the product of the discourses circulating at that time. This new positivity is now due for quite a long run, and has effectively displaced statements like 'Cook discovered Australia'. However, such a statement is not just the attainment of a new truth (something which only fools and bigots would dare deny), for there are no truths waiting 'out there' to be discovered, accumulated and repeated. The statement about Aboriginal resistance appears as part of a social formation which is operating *now*; it is closely tied up with the Aboriginal political claim to sovereignty and the desire to express a militant resolve among Aboriginal activists and their white allies.

How, then, shall we write the history of Roebuck Plains? The following represent some alternatives, intended only to be suggestive.

GREAT INDIVIDUALS:
Traditionally, history is about kings. King William III was so impressed with Dampier's account of his first voyage to New Holland, published in 1697, that he sent him on a second trip ...

GREAT INDIVIDUALS II:
The history of Roebuck Plains could be centred around Paddy Roe, who

was the first person of Aboriginal descent in the Broome region to have a driver's licence. He is said to have blood connections with the pioneering Roe family of Western Australia:

> One of Clara's descendents,[73] Paddy Roe, is an important figure in north-west Australian Aboriginal society, a law man and storyteller with responsibility for initiating young boys into his still-living Aboriginal culture. He recently published a book of his stories Gularbulu—the Coast where the Sun Goes Down [sic] and is working on another.[74]

SOVEREIGNTY, PROPER NAMES, NUMBERS IN TIME AND SPACE:

A detail from a Western Australian Surveyor General's map of 1884 (public plan 6K). From historical records it would appear to be the first official European map of the Roebuck Plains area.

146

It is significant that the archival discourse establishing European owner-ship of the Plains is underpinned by selections which are typically absent from the Aboriginal discourse which maintains its sovereignty over the land. In Aboriginal discourse the land and its 'owners' are not subject to a single higher authority (the 'crown'), land is not invested in someone's (proper) name and ownership is not quantified over a given period (the lease) or a given area.

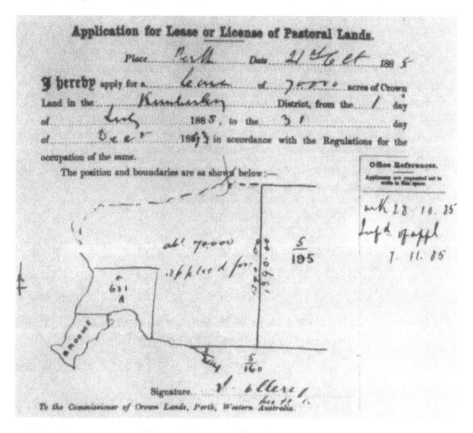

'Ownership', in the Aboriginal sense, is circumscribed by extensive and intimate knowledge of particular places. Individuals who function as guardians of these places do so only by virtue of the knowledges they hold about the land. The land is not attached to their names; they, as individuals or clan groups are instead identified with the names of the country.

In the white discourse the land has only one name and it is a varying quantity put to the service of a succession of sovereign owners, starting with the Queen:

PASTORAL LEASE

Elizabeth the Second, by the Grace of God, of the United Kingdom, Australia and her other Realms and Territories, Queen, Head of the Commonwealth, Defender of the Faith. To all to whom these Presents shall come, Greeting: Know Ye that We of our especial Grace and in exercise of the powers in this behalf to Us given by the Land Act, 1933, and Amendments do by these presents lease to ... [proper name] ... hereinafter called 'the Lessee' which term includes the Lessee, his executors, administrators, and assigns the natural surface of all that piece or parcel of land situated in the district of ... Dampier ... and containing ... [number] ... acres as delineated by a border of green colour on the plan herein: To hold onto the said Lessee for pastoral purposes under and subject to the provisions of Part VI of the said Act and except as hereinafter provided, for the term of ... [number] ... years ... [number] ... months ... [number] ... days to be computed from the ... [date] ... until ... [date] ...

Lease No.	Date	Lessee	Acreage
5/223 — 5/195	1885-1890	James Henry ELLERY	170,000
71/178	1890-1900	Edwin William STREETER	170,000
277/98	1900-1918	George Skelton STREETER	443,000
1125/9875	1918-1931	George Skelton STREETER	1,000,000
	1931-1936	Blanche STREETER	
		Thomas Thornton STREETER	
		John Skelton STREETER	717,851
	1936-1951	Blanche STREETER	
		Thomas Thornton STREETER	717,851
396/441	1951-19	William SKULTHORP	717,851
	1953-1962	George Ernest HARRIS	
		Winifrede Leah HARRIS	
		Patrick Ronald HARRIS	
		Ernest Thomas Lionel HARRIS	970,291
3114/499	1962-1974	Eileen Violet HAMLETT	
		Frank James HAMLETT	720,579
	1974-	Roebuck Plains Holdings Pty Ltd	715,346

CAUSE AND EFFECT:
The Nyigina people first arrived in Roebuck Plains to occupy camping spots left vacant by the previously resident Yawur and Djugun people who had been attracted by the bright lights of Broome and the possibility of gaining employment there.

CAUSE AND EFFECT II:
The Yawur and Djugun people resisted the occupation of their lands by settlers, but their numbers were already severely depleted because of blackbirding for the pearling fleets. Men and women who had been blackbirded often never came back home because when they were laid off the boats they could be killed in hostile territory by other tribes. Disease and poison were also killing people around the country, so it was often safer to move into Broome.

ECONOMICS:

> *Streeter was the first to realize that money could be earned quickly at this land base* [for the pearling fleet] *and he employed George Roe, son of the first Surveyor General,*[76] *to erect his store and residence with Alf Gummow of T.I. then contracted to build the Roebuck Arms for Streeter and this he sub-leased, after obtaining his licence at Derby. Aware of the demand for fresh meat, Streeter then took up a pastoral lease which he called Roebuck Downs to supply his butcher shop. This was so successful that when some of the pearlers' wives came to Broome, he established and leased a dairy and milk run.*[77]

ECONOMICS II:

Before the white fellas   no station nothing   no station just, just the country   oh mighta been some sorta station some other place   'cos Roebuck Plain didn' have station   nothing   but Roebuck Plain station was in diff'ren' place in ah top Lumangan, Lumangan Station, that further
up in Derby Road   then they come back an' build this one then.
Stephen: Roebuck Plains?
Roebuck Plains.

Stephen: Who was the first person to make that?
Roebuck Plains, . I dunno.
Stephen: Males?

No   might beee Streeter.
Stephen: Oh yeah.
Streeter, Streeters, that's a Streeter Station.
Stephen: First time?
First time.
Stephen: After that you got.
Male, Male   then they come together Streeter and Male   two man
little bit more this one (Gestures 'money') you know.
Krim: Together, yeah.
Mix up, Streeter and Male   then when Streeter finish   Male took over
everything   Male   sheep camp   Roebuck Plains that's the cattle
Station   head station   sheep camp's only more like an out camp
you know.

Stephen: And after that you got Roe, maybe?
Ah only just passing by might be.
Stephen: Oh, I see.
He never stay in the station   Thangoo   he only had Thangoo.
Stephen: He was owner for that.
Owner.

Stephen: Well who took over Roebuck Plains after Male?
Aah Ronans   he's a bloke from Queensland, Ronan   that's after.[78]
Stephen: You worked with him at the sheep camp?
No, but I bin born already then.
Stephen: Who did you have after Ronan?
Ah Ronan an' then Mr Evans   Mr Evans?
Stephen: Yeah.

Ah, from there Mr Cole   I dunno what his other name   Mr Cole an'
then   who was the other fella?   Oh Mr Cole and them in my
time then   I was little boy already riding horse   the other fellas was
then   oh lotta people bin there you know   changing   one sell the
station 'nother fella come in 'nother one sell station 'nother fella gone
'nother one come in 'nother one gone 'nother one come in.
Krim: Lots of bosses.
An' today it's diff'ren' again now.

*Krim: How much did your people get paid on the station in the early
days?*

Few sticks o' tobacco my people used to get an' box o' matches
every week they get   that's the wage.

Krim: Like ration.
Ration   only sticks of tobacco and everything but tucker we all eat, one.
Krim: Soap, you get?
Soap, every week.
Krim: Yeah, ration.
Ration, yeah   might be nearly big as this one you know (Gestures) might be cut 'im in half for two man *(Laughter)* wash clothes you know.
Krim: And could you own a horse or anything?
Nothing   nothing   so   when all our   nothing   we had NOTHING for ourselves. We done EVERYthing for the station, we get nothing.
Krim: Yeah.

We, we was happy too   the way we used to live, because money is nothing to us   we er   sometime we come into town   we get about five shillings a year   we come into picture, boss used to tell us we can go into picture now.
Krim: Yeah.
Oh young people, you know, old people never worry   so we get five shilling each and we spend about three shilling in town, go to pictures, cool drink shop, lollies, anything we buy or whatever, bun, jam tart, you know they all ha'penny or penny (Laugh) plenty tucker.
Krim: What's that, once a month you go to picture or —once a year?
Once a year.
Krim: Once a year (Laughter).
But we still come back with two bob (Laugh) can't spend it   too much tucker for three shilling too (Laughter).

Krim: Ah, good one, but the other thing is, maybe the boss make a lot of money.
Ah yeah, lot of money.
Krim: But the workers they …
Nothing, we work for nothing.
Krim: Yeah that's it, one become rich, the other, nothing.
Nothing yeah, that's true   well that's the first thing anyway that's the thing   they used to do to us.
Krim: Did you know that? Did the people talk about it among themselves?
Eeer we used to talk about it but ah   we used to talk about this too but ah we was quite happy too.
Krim: Yeah.
We was quite happy long as we get some tucker and all these sort of

151

things   when we go out for holiday then we get ration every week
jam flour tea sugar   if we want a bullock then the boss shoot a bullock
and we can do what we like with 'im   it's a thing like that.
Krim: That's fair enough.
But er we never really worry about the money, those days you know,
more like to us the money was nothing to us, where we goin' to spend
it? What we goin' to spend it on?   We didn't know, you know.
Krim: Yeah.
Because we never   well really the station people we never really come
to town.
Krim: Yeah, much.
Much you know   soon as we come into town we gotta pull out
money all the time   but we ...

*Krim: Maybe even money that time was not very important —because
now you need money to get things.*
True, now.
Krim: Everything depend on money but then.
That's right.
Krim: Before you know it's all right you know.
It's all right.
Krim: People were simple.
Yeah.
Krim: Just have a bit of tucker.
Tucker.
Krim: Clothes and ...
Clothes   we happy.
Krim: Yeah, today cars, boats, houses.
Yeah   everything   petrol we gotta look for all the time.
Krim: Petrol.
Tyres.
Krim: Yeah all the ...
Oil everything   we must have money, today.
Krim: Yeah.
But before we never worry.
*Krim: (Laugh) Yeah but now become worried, think 'Ah, but I didn't
make bit of money before' (Laughter).*

Yeah.
*Krim: That's the problem now for Aboriginal people because before
they*
*didn't get no money —station people, you know, bosses make a lot of
money.*

152

Lot of money.
Krim: And Aboriginal people nothing.
Mm that's right.

Oh I used to do everything I put up the windmill, tank, trough   at the
station you know for that   for the same thing and   every year I used
to shear the sheep we had about oh   little bit over eleven hundred
sheep.
Mm.
All the time 'round there you know   over eleven hundred, er eleven
thousand.
Krim: Eleven thousand.
Eleven thousand   sheep   we had there so I used to shear all them
might be little bit more, over eleven thousand anyway   but every year I
gotta shear them too, me an my boss   blade shear.
Krim: Yeah (Laugh).

So we never worry anything anyway those days but now we   'cos
'nother thing too we didn' have much English to eer.
Krim: To argue.
To   eer yeah because we was quite satisfied with the bosses we thought
that was the right thing.
Krim: Yeah.
Long as we get boots an' hat an' clothes an' everything well eeer
something you know   that's it (Laughter) and er   we never think
about   er this man must be getting more rich than us, no   nobody
never think about.
*Krim: And did you leave the job when you want to, I mean when you're
sick of the job?*
Oh well we ask the boss, 'I finish now here, I gotta move 'nother station'
some people used to go, but they wouldn't let me go   I used to ask my
boss, 'I want to finish I gotta go to 'nother station now, you know' you
know, I say and er 'I bin here little bit too long, on the same job you
know'.
Krim: Yeah.
I try look for diff'ren' job   'We can't let you go' (Laughter)   so I
used to run away.

Krim: And they get you back, or you come back or ...?
They just wait around, 'Where's Paddy?'   'Oh he's workin' in that
station'
Ah, come night time you see the boss there, 'Is he here?'   'Yeah'   Ah,
he go 'round, you see (Grabs Krim's arm, laughter) 'Come on'.

Krim: Come on (Laughter).
'You better come with me, you all right?' (With surprise) 'Oh! Yeah.'
Krim: And did you feel like you weren't free? You know when boss comes and take you back?
Aaah not really, not really, I never get that way too because 'nother thing I used to worry about my country too, I don't like to leave-im (Laughter)   you know?
Krim: Yeah.
I'm happy and then I get little bit more, close, more close together (Laughter)   you see?
Krim: Yeah. They look after you more.
They look after me more.
Krim: Oh good one yes.

You know   mm   anything I ask for I got-im (Laughter) you know yeah yeah   my people might come somewhere, 'Oh I got some people over there in the camp my people just come from bush, I want a bag o' flour, tea, sugar   bullock meat, you know, salt meat an' everything' 'Yeah yeah yeah, bring-em up,' my uncles and brothers and all these fellas from bush.
Krim: Yeah, just don't run away we give you what you want (Laughter).
So we bring these fellas, they got no clothes, trousers, anything, just come with their *narga*, you know.
Krim: Yeah (Laughter).
Walk into station carry their flour and off they go.
Krim: You can get them jobs too if they want?
If they want to he can get them job   but er we had 'nuff people there you know but just ME they couldn't let me go but the others they never worry they   just couldn't let ME go   one man (Laugh) you know.

Krim: Because you were a good worker.
Good worker that's right and understand too I understand everything I
can run the place an' all that too you know   and I can talk to my people too   we used to get some people, you know   but eeer well   to hold me there I s'pose because not just because boss like to give tucker to these fellas you know and er no work.

Krim: Yeah.
But they   er   must please me.
Krim: Yeah I see, what, you were the boss of the workers there.
Workers yeah.
Krim: Organise them and everything you know.

154

Yeah I can talk little bit English.

Krim: Yeah.

Well I can talk English, I can understand what boss tell me and I tell my boys in language   'Ooh yeah', get the shovel and crowbar, off we go, put the fence up (Laughter) happy, you know.

Krim: Oh that's good.

Good old life those days too.

Minimum/Maximum

We must therefore learn to judge a society on the basis of its
sounds, on its art and its festivals rather than on its statistics.
It is by listening to sounds that we can better understand how
far the madness of men and their accounts has driven us, and
what hopes are still real possibilities.

Jacques Attali.

Of all the noises that our society makes, economics is now among the loudest. Everyone is speaking about inflation, unemployment, taxes, prices and wages. The truth of the matter is that over the last ten years the world economy has been slowing down and growth is virtually at an end.

Western Australia, and the companies which mine there, are struggling to maintain revenue and growth in the North-West by the extraction of natural resources: gas, oil, diamonds, pearl shell, cultured pearls. As, it appears (figures are, of course, not provided), most of the profits from these ventures are exported, and not reinvested in the local community, the maintenance of a town like Broome is a drain on the general Australian economy. The 'taxpayer' has to pay for unemployment and other welfare benefits, the running of a hospital, a prison and a post office, the erection and maintenance of state housing, and so on.

So, in spite of an appearance of pioneering growth in the region, the economy has in fact stagnated along with the rest of the world. The zero-growth rate, for which ecologists used to clamour in vain, is here, but without the degradation of the environment having yet ceased. And in a situation of massive unemployment and reduction of revenues, nobody is particularly happy.

Certain Broome people, the descendants of the nomadic tribes, maintain a certain part of their production and consumption at a local level, outside of the capitalist economy. This involves hunting, fishing and gathering locally available foods which are distributed in the community.

157

Some people could still survive on the traditional whitefella rations of flour, tea and sugar if these were supplemented with the local catch.

It is this *supplement* which creates a *distinction* of pleasure and profit for the locals. It cuts across or subverts the standard capitalist manner of acquiring profits: investment of money, controlling the means of production, exploiting labour to the advantage of capital. In benefitting from the free gifts of the land (gifts which are nonetheless the product of local knowledge, skill, energy and technology) the nomad gains a subversive profit which is the envy of every tourist. This potential cutting of corners in relation to the economy has an attraction for this other sort of nomad—the ones who bring their caravans along with them.

But even if the tourist is lumbered with a caravan, and can't always find the good fishing spots, there are still always free gifts being offered by the country, gifts which repay one's sympathetic attention. The *ngadjayi*, the water-nymphs who leap from the breaking waves only making themselves visible for a split second in the corner of one's eye—perhaps only revealing themselves fully to the *maban*, the people who would not be too shocked to see them, remain, apparently, at a spot on Roebuck Plains where the sea once lapped the shore.

And if you are driving north from Port Hedland towards Broome, there is a point where the scrub is low, with broad silver leaves almost twinkling in the bright sunlight. Suddenly a flock of budgerigars passes over the flat scrub: a fast green cloud, they wheel and turn, it changes to blue.

The nomad gathers huge amounts of whatever is available and shares with the community in the appropriate manner; as long as supplies don't run out, the people can gorge themselves to the maximum. Where there are no refrigerators there is no ideology of 'saving for a rainy day' (this austerity has its modern manifestation in the governmental messages which urge us to 'tighten our belts', 'work together for the good of the country', etc.).

When supplies run out, the people might go hungry, subsisting on a minimum of food or water. Consumption tends to oscillate between these two poles of minimum and maximum, desire and satisfaction. It is not interrupted by mechanisms which control the flow of consumer products. It escapes what Krim calls (he is a celebrated chef as well as an artist) 'portion control', the effects of which are strongly felt in kitchens north of the twenty-sixth parallel: 'No, you're giving them too much—a bit of this and a portion of that'. A dab of butter, minutely wrapped, a little container of jam. No minimum, no maximum. Derisory amounts for someone trying to bring up a tribe of children.

Portion control facilitates accounting in motels and hotels since a 1:1 relationship can be established between each client and the portions which are given to them each day. Their room is their daily portion of space, various well-defined needs are portioned out each day in exchange for their portion of cash, from which the government has taxed its portion, and so on.

Even the English language (the language of the 'nation of shopkeepers') has built into it, in what are called binominal expressions, an ideology of portion control: *cup of* tea (sugar, flour etc.); *packet of ...,* *crate of ...,* *handful of ...* Although Aboriginal languages have names for parts of animals or plants, they do not have expressions which divide a mass of goods into arbitrarily-sized portions.

Portion control is a product of factory technologies and the tricks of accountants in the service of business. While the production end of business reaches out for the maximum in profits, the consumer side of the market is subjected to the petty and depressing effect of the airlines lunch. A minimum of pleasure, just enough to keep you 'happy.'

No doubt the consumer of pettiness finds his or her maximum/minimum in other areas of life, but the nomad knows it in everything and the country is the final arbiter; it sends a school of salmon or just one or two. It sends a big mob of *barni* or just a little lizard.

Barra djiburr-djiburr rranggarran djida
Sunrise   bird   dawn   light

rra-rra rarrdjali njina
look around PLACE ———

Fishermen's Bend II

1983, 57 cm x 61.5 cm, gouache and pastel on D'Arches paper

Rediscovery

Williams, who had laboured *so hard since his* return to Australia *to find the* appropriate form *for* the *landscape, had now found a mode which* rediscovered *the Australian* bush, *making from the discovery a painting on an* epic *scale yet retaining the* personal *quality of his handling. This new form was* believable, *because it came from* experience. *It was not wished or willed upon the landscape but derived from it. He had found a* geometry *for nature, for the* untidy, straggly, unpicturesque *bush. He had* ordered *his* experience.[79]

I would like to make this quotation from Patrick McCaughey's book on Fred Williams the subject of a small meditation on the ideology of art criticism, an ideology which is anti-nomadic and prevents us from reading Krim's paintings, and is quite unrelated to the debt that Krim has to Williams' work. I have emphasised those words which stand out as the *givens* of this discourse, the assumptions which align with dominant ideas on culture and life and have nothing necessarily to do with art.

Firstly, whatever the other conditions which make an artist's work possible, it is important that he or she *work hard* to achieve a certain goal. It is not enough, in the ideology which McCaughey is projecting, just to want to paint, or to paint because that is all one can do. Labour value, it is assumed, is an accepted part of the value of the aesthetic product.

Next, in the trajectory of the artist's career which McCaughey is mapping, Williams has just returned to Australia (Chapter Four) and is about to embark upon 'Maturity' (Chapter Five). The passage quoted, at the end of Chapter Four, established the preconditions for the mature landscape painter, presumably all landscape painters. In the fifties and sixties the European experience was an essential part of the training of the Australian cultural elite. It was a transformatory experience: 'Fred Williams left as a student and returned, early in 1957, an artist'. 80 In this myth of the departure and the return of the artist is a whole series of assumptions about the necessity of just this operation, this migration to the 'home countries'. No matter what one did 'over there', it is important to *come back* and re-establish one's Australian credentials.

It is then important to work on Australian materials. What could be more Australian than the country which bears that name? But Williams had no particular penchant for the bush. In fact he revealed to a scandalised press in 1982, [81] before his death, that he 'couldn't stand' being out there, that he would spend a couple of hours working in the field before hiking back to his studio where he could work on the real subject of his paintings, the problem of landscape painting in Australia. The suggestion that he might not love what he is supposed to be representing cuts into the assumption written into McCaughey's text that the business of the landscape painter is to do something affective with the bush. Rediscover it, in fact.

The 'bush' is the unspoken content for landscape painting. Williams' task is to find the 'appropriate form' to carry this always-present content. In the extract the critic makes explicit his belief that the artist derives everything from the landscape/bush (the terms are sometimes interchangeable). His experience in the bush becomes the content of his paintings, just as Australian literature is supposed to be in many cases read as the profound relation between a pioneering (discovering) sensibility and the country. The myth of the bush or the 'great interior' depends, firstly, on an assumption about its singularity ('the' landscape). What would happen to this myth if critics had to find quite distinct meanings for different parts of the bush? Doesn't the discourse depend as much on a monolithic conception of 'the bush' as it does on an assumption about the singular and undivided artistic gaze which the individual artist brings to bear on it? Secondly, the myth depends on assumptions about the divergent nature of 'the bush'. For the urban and European critic there is something wrong with this bush. It is *untidy, straggly* and *unpicturesque*. (According to Webster's dictionary, 'picturesque' means 'representing with the clearness of ideal beauty appropriate to a picture'.) It doesn't already look like a picture because it isn't like a European landscape (Saul Bellow had a character in one of his novels, who found he couldn't look out of the window of a train in the Swiss Alps because all he could see were chocolate-box illustrations). This wayward and undesirable landscape has to be ordered by the *precision* of a *geometry*. It has to be brought into line like a rebellious schoolboy, with the knowledge of ages.

The critic cannot be wrong be because he is projecting responsible, mature, middle-class urban beliefs onto something which stands no chance of contradicting him: an abstracted canvas. What if Williams' *You Yangs* series, which McCaughey is discussing, lacked geometry? What if all those splashes were considered wayward and untidy? Certainly, at first showing, *You Yangs 1* 'didn't measure up' according to the critics, [82] and I think the word 'measure' is significant here.

The trace as writing

Krim's painting Garrigarrigabu' (page 43), denies respectable recuperation with one word *merde* extending vertically on a pencil line. Written on the bare canvas it inscribes a complex attitude on beginning a painting (the word is also used among French thespians on opening night to wish each other good luck). It may also generate an intertextual effect with Robert Juniper's graffiti canvases. Juniper's obscenities on canvas are a post-respectability allowance. But Krim is not copying a form, he is using *writing* in his painting, he is tracing a limit of representation which is other than that of colour and form. This limit is brought into focus when his lyrical *merde* is found to be not the only bit of writing on the canvas: on another vertical, opposed to the capitals is something like a scrawl, also extending vertically, something like what school children used to call 'running writing'. This trace, which is more than just a squiggle is guided by a hand, and *connotes* 'writing'. Its force, as illegibility, is of the same order as the unacceptability of *merde,* though that word is completely legible, and fainter.

This paradoxical development of the trace relates to a *direction* in the painting which is quite other than respectability. As Roland Barthes says of writing in Cy Twombly's paintings:

> ... the trace, however supple, light or uncertain it is, is always related to a force, to a direction. It is an energon, a moment of work, which enables one to read it as a drive and as a spilling forth. The trace is visible action.[83]

There is yet another trace in this painting which speaks of writing, of the discrete sign in a semiotic space which is other than that of the country represented. It is the ideogram, the confident initialled signature on the lower right of the spring. It doubles the centrality of the major spring by being the juxtaposed symbol of *the trace as writing* which is the painting's other theme. In the other paintings there is the trace as *line* (as pure form), the trace as *track,* and the trace as *boundary.* Here the trace as boundary becomes the trace as writing, since, compared to the painting 'Djarrmanggunan—second sheep camp' (page 54), the fence is displaced and becomes coterminous with the horizon, and the paddock fence around the spring is effaced and becomes just this kind of trace.

This erasure (a condition of writing, tracks and other traces is their potential for eventual erasure) finds its support in the turbulent fluidity of the spread of colour. The colours, instead of being fixed and localised like minerals in the sand in 'Djarrmanggunan—second sheep camp' are now melting and in a state of flux. They are either coming or going like the Roebuck Plains dawns and sunsets. This painting, or rather the significance of this painting as I see it, swings on the paradox of present-but-absent. The familiar barbed wire fence can't really be there, superimposed on the horizon. Its absence gives a 'normal' landscape, but it joins, in its presence, the traces as writing (which are really 'absent' or erased fences). The signature initial next to the spring is absent (is it a 'P'?) as writing. As a letter-ideogram it is halfway between the line and the alphabet. What it does *not* fully inscribe is a tree in the landscape, one just like the others, but not fully coloured in. In this it joins the sketch of the spring lower left which is there but not there. The paradox of this painting lies in its deconstruction of its own origins. It cuts the ground away from what was established in 'Djarrmanggunan—second sheep camp'. It shows its own *brouillons,* its beginnings as a sketch. Trace as form gives way to trace as writing, and the first and final comment is *merde,* in all its ambiguity.

Play

The painting 'Fisherman's Bend III' (page 167) also exploits the trace as writing, though in a way coherent with the 'play' of the painting. One of the Fisherman's Bend series, it repeats the fantastic spotted animals, of which one might be a crab. One animal (a turtle?) is emerging from its traces, its tracks which give it form. Its spots have appeared first but we can still see through the transparent head to the horizon. The whole painting is thus in a stage of *emergence,* in a state of play, or rather 'playing'. (Our game is one in which we invent animals on the beach, as European kids invent castles. It is like the mud animals of Paddy and Joe at *Djarmanggunan,* playing at *bugarrigarra,* at the creation of animals from the country in the dreamtime.)

The traces which are going to be the turtle merge also into a word: *Dune* or *sure?* (Shore?) This time the writing is ambiguous but representative of what is represented. It *plays* with the idea of representation by *labelling* the thing you might be seeing in the painting: a dune on a shore. But can you be sure about what you are seeing? The trace from the word runs into and becomes something that might become an animal if it emerged more. As it is, it represents an abstract notion of these kinds of animals, which, as we shall see, are of a special kind. Its tail trails away on two pompoms of colour; a whimsical touch; but one which is repeated on the other side of the canvas where the idea of animal is represented in an even more minimal way: a trace, a squiggle and a colour (a red splash). Animal is thus 'written'. But there is even more writing at the bottom of the canvas. Head and tail disappear and on the left the writing suggests the Arabic script of Krim's youth, while on the right this fragments even further. What kind of animals are we dealing with? Turtles, sea-snakes, crabs and shellfish, they are all of the ambiguous sort which belong both to the land and the sea. They are figures which join land and sea, fantasy and reality, images and writing, absence and presence. The paradox of there and not there is the paradox of nomadism. Forms are always in a state of emergence, a state of play. Krim had no intention, to pick up Patrick McCaughey's phrase again, of 'ordering his experience'. This painting has nothing to do with his experience, unless it is his experience at an unconscious level. The event most closely tied to the production of this painting is its sensual articulation with Krim's body: his use of palette knives, brushes, thumbs and fingernails. He is no more committed to the reality of his experience in 'the bush' than Paddy Roe is to the 'reality' of the *bugarrigarra*. What then becomes important, when the realist obsession falls away, is the manner of painting for pleasure and the way of storytelling the pleasure. This is not to say that Paddy Roe doesn't care about the *bugarrigarra*, rather that the critic doesn't need to tell him that his understanding of it is 'believable'. Believable for whom?

This brings up the whole question of the use of criticism. Criticism should prise open the multiple ways in which a work can be read rather than showing it to be 'ordered'. Critics should give artists ideas for their next picture, not just say whether they like or dislike what they have done in terms of the most general and acceptable middle-class values.

Fishermen's Bend III

1983, 56.5 cm x 60.5 cm, gouache and pastel on D 'Arches paper

Bricolage

The bricoleur, *says Levi-Strauss, is someone who uses 'the means at hand', that is, the instruments he finds at his disposition around him, those which are already there, which had not been especially concerned with an eye to the operation for which they are to be used and to which one tries by trial and error to adapt them, not hesitating to change them whenever it appears necessary ...*

Derrida.

Bricolage could be called the activity of roaming in the ruins of a culture, picking up useful bits and pieces to keep things going or even make them function better. The opposite, it has been suggested, would be engineering, the achievements of which seem to stand alone, made out of nothing deriving from the past.

But something can't be made out of nothing, so the engineer's products (like the 1984 Holden) are just *illusions of immaculate conceptions*. Roland Barthes described cars in just these terms:

> *I think that cars today are almost the exact equivalent of the great Gothic cathedrals: I mean the supreme creation of an era, conceived with passion by unknown artists and consumed in image if not in usage by a whole population which appropriates them as a purely magical object.*[84]

Of course the magic, the illusion, is shattered when cars become subject to *bricolage* (that is, customising). A wire coat-hanger appears as a substitute for the aerial and suddenly the mystical object becomes a plain functional machine. *Bricolage* becomes visible when we can *trace* the origins of the different pieces making up the whole.

This is more difficult for the new and intact car, but still possible. The car was conceived as a *bricolage* of last year's design, European and American influences, new gadgets and fashionable colours. By tracing back these parts to their 'sources' we can begin to understand the significance of the object.

Bricolage destroys the mystique of the engineer, precisely by showing that the only 'true' engineer would be a god—someone who can create things from nothing, someone whose products can't be traced through historical traditions. Beyond this, *bricolage* is a practice, a way of living which is creative and economical. The *anti-bricoleur* throws away a shirt if it loses a button and buys a new one. The *bricoleur* is happy to sew on a different button.

Aboriginal *bricoleurs,* often through necessity, used barbed wire as clothes lines; forty-four gallon drums three-quarters full of sand make excellent fireplaces, and kerosene is a most efficient way of starting a fire, a method which would not be used by those brought up within the austerity of a Baden-Powell ideology, according to which one match should suffice.

Given the choice, Aboriginal people would without doubt choose a gas fire and a proper clothes line with pegs. A celebration of adaptive practices like *bricolage* should not detract from the fact that, as a class, these people have always suffered the highest rate of unemployment, the worst health, and the most inadequate living conditions since the arrival of European settlers in Australia turned survival strategies completely around. From that moment, survival for Aboriginal people has been *forced* into the no-man's-land of *bricolage*. Instantaneous assimilation was just as much out of the question as totally ignoring white culture, pretending it wasn't there. The only other position was the fluid fringe-dwelling position which demanded the constant practice of *bricolage*.

Bricolage as a way of life is flexible and adaptive and it is present in all cultures. It can even be seen as subversive of the dominant culture. The word *bricolage* has been used to explain the emergence of the phenomena of punk and Teddy boy fashions in Britain in the 'pop' era:

> ... *the Teddy boy's theft and transformation of the Edwardian style revived in the early 1950s by Saville Row for wealthy young men about town can be construed as an act of* bricolage. *Similarly the mods could be said to be functioning as* bricoleurs *when they appropriated another range of commodities by placing them in a symbolic ensemble which served to erase or subvert their original straight meanings ... the motor scooter, originally an ultra-respectable means of transport, was turned into a menacing symbol of group solidarity. In the same improvisatory manner, metal combs, honed to a razor-like sharpness, turned narcissism into an offensive weapon. Union Jacks were emblazoned on the backs of grubby parka anoraks or cut up and converted into smartly tailored jackets.*[85]

Similarly, though not necessarily with the, intention to subvert, second-hand charity clothes which arrive in isolated Aboriginal communities are used for their practical value (checked dressing-gowns are worn to guard against the wind at any time of day or night) or generate their own fashions within that community; in one instance plastic mixing bowls became a headwear fashion among the women.

Even remotely isolated Aboriginal communities are aware of the codes of modern fashions; it is difficult to know to what extent the wearing of clothes in the 'wrong way' is an expression of disregard for the dominant culture for there are also preferred colours and patterns which tie in with more traditional cultural forms. In any case it would seem that fashion in Aboriginal communities obeys its own internal rules on the one hand, and on the other is a function of the availability of the materials.

One image which is endlessly repeated in white representations of blacks is that of the black abandoning the external trappings of white culture and 'going back to a natural state'. Especially shoes: in a Ted Egan song a young man from the Northern Territory throws away his purple jacket and platform shoes from Carnaby Street and sings:

> *Oh give me flour and tea*
> *and jam and sugar*
> *and a plug of nikki-nikki too ...*

(as if to say; 'to hell with the individual achievement of dominant Western culture, give me back the feudalism and pastoral care of the era of rations and slave-labour'). Similarly a video clip of a David Bowie song ('Let's dance') shows an Aboriginal woman trampling on the red shoes she bought in Sydney and 'going back' to the idyll of country life.

These sorts of images are made possible only because of a romantic European misconception of 'the country' (where one is at peace and living in harmony with nature). Life is tough for blacks in country towns where in an intimate society they have to suffer daily onslaughts of racism (as Peter Yu points out in the interview on page 229).

A displacement towards traditional society is equally misleading. Discarding Western clothing does not reduce one to a state of nature; it is an *exchange*. Nakedness or semi-nakedness is also a kind of fashionable dressing. Apart from traditional possum-fur pubic covers, hair belts, decorations and so on, there is a sense of belonging to a culture through the wearing or not wearing of *just those things*.

But the *bricoleur* never exchanges one set of meanings completely for another. He or she leaves the two representations half complete. (Again the early images of 'natives' wearing full formal Western attire, but with bare feet.) *Bricolage* is thus disruptive of what we expect to always perceive as 'the normal'. It ruptures continuities in the same way that the Charlie Chaplin film camera can cause an audience to erupt into laughter as it pans across a completely normal scene until it discovers an anomalous detail.

170

In a similar way Paddy Roe's storytelling, as it has been written down here, stands as a *bricolage* of standard English and Aboriginal languages. In spite of the fluency and the richness of the expressive possibilities of Paddy Roe's speech, it is all too easy to make two errors in reading it. One is the familiar mistake of seeing Aboriginal English as a 'bastard' version of standard English; language fallen from grace. Such an attitude is supported by a traditional purist condemnation of any powerless varieties of English like the migrant Englishes or youth subculture styles. These varieties lack the support of institutions like the ABC, dictionaries and grammars. The other error would be to overcorrect it in writing it down, to produce a language which doesn't indicate strongly enough that it is different from standard English. Not only does Paddy Roe have things to say which are not normally expressed in standard English, but in a sense his *way* of expressing them gives them their meaning. The repetitions, the voice inflections and the gestures are all part of a style which is recognisable right across Aboriginal Australia. To edit them out would be to banish the Aboriginality from the texts. If the texts then present some difficulty for 'the general reader' (whatever that is), then all the better. *Bricolage*, in any form, sets up a double vision, it forces a juxtaposition of forms, and new meanings must emerge. The one reader who is not disadvantaged is the Aboriginal reader, who, familiar with the conventions and forms, can easily reconstruct a fuller spoken narrative from the text.

But for both Aboriginal and 'general' readers there is a pleasure in the text of *bricolage,* a pleasure in seeing the edifice of language tremble a little as it becomes a kind of poetry. *Bricolage* is flexible, economical and unstable. It does not seek continuity or harmony in a world of discontinuity and inequality. It is functional rather than idealistic; it uses the wrong object for a useful purpose, but can change according to necessity. It suffers no illusions. It allows a goat to make her home in an abandoned car.

Danggu warra danggu guwawara-wara
jaw (hand on) jaw   ———

irrnginji-nginji mililjinj ingandjin-yana
PLACE   finger-like   he lies down

BIYARRUGAN

Bugarrigarra bin leave-im name   and that 'nother one   *Marriyangarda*
same   he nothing   only *bugarrigarra* bin leave 'is name.[86]

But in the end   right up in end of that hill   there's the hill now that
little red hill, you see-im right up in this, this is a flat runs right up
right up   halfway there   well other side of that he's a scrub   well
that's where my old father's spirit lives all the time, today too.

Ray: That's your father's brother or your father?
No my, father   not   not his brother   my father.
Ray: Your father, that's his spirit.
That's his spirit, he lives there today.
Ray: Up near that flat scrub country.
Yeah.
Oh big, big clay pans there too you know   billabongs, big ones, two
each side   that place called *Djarrigabu* and *Yanjgayinanj.*

174

Ray: That's those two places.
Well the old fella live in there between those two waterholes   big hill
in the scrub, country, that way.

Ray: You wanta go there or not?
Can't get through   no road.

Now you can see this hill in Jerricop, *Biyarrugan*   that's the proper
Biyarrugan, ah hill   that hill bin there.

He walked away from there and there he is   today   he moved away, to
that one.
Ray: Right.

But he bin there for   I couldn't tell you how many years   for years an'
years   from *bugarrigarra*   but he bin move   but he bin move this
time.
Ray: That's that fellow again?
Eh?
Ray: That's that fellow from bugarrigarra?
Yeah.
Ray: He moved around from that one to that one?
Yeah, he moved from there   that's the proper hill that was very high
hill   wind come he blow him away he walk away to there now   to
there now, little one   through here.

But in my time when I used to work in the stock-camp   here   that one
never had hill.
Ray: Aah.
All plain like this one.
Ray: Yeah, an' he flew.
He moved after we left   Oh I left the country too   an' other people,
well all died you see   I left the country an' these things moved away
you can see now too   but that hill was up there on top o' that one.
Ray: Yeah.
When we climb up ooh we got very tired climbing up   that hill.

Now   how that hill got there that big high hill   that was a, woman
woman   used to come for tucker from Crab Creek   pick up tucker all
the time 'round this country   one woman.

Eer tucker we call *yarinyari* he dig in the ground you know   like a
onion, little one.

An' two man come from this side   that was   two man an' when
this woman seen these two man come up they come from this side   he
never seen man before   he look very funny, to this woman   an' this
two man come more close an' close they see this woman very funny too
(Laugh)   they never seen a woman before   an' they want to come
very close to 'im just want to touch 'im that woman turn into hill
that's the hill was standing there now long way   that's the woman
and finish   two man too   two man fly away they're brolga today
bird, but they bin man   *bugarrigarra.*

Yeah today that two man is brolga now they digging here now for that
tucker   when brolga time   er this time now   come in the morning
here you see brolga everywhere, digging.

Lawdarra   yarabana gunardangana
Brolga (she) saw them moving way up ahead

　　　buyu warra ngindjing
　　　long way　　　————

My Body, This Song, This Fire

The warm sense of well-being arising from physical love must have been transferred into many primitive experiences. To set fire to the stick by sliding it up and down in the groove- in the piece of dry wood takes time and patience. But this work must have been very agreeable to an individual whose reverie was wholly sexual. It was perhaps while engaged in this gentle task that man learned to sing. In any case it is an obviously rhythmic kind of task, a task which answers to the rhythm of the worker, which brings him lovely, multiple resonances; the arm that rubs, the pieces of wood that strike together, the voice that sings, all are united in the same harmony and the same rhythmic increase in energy; everything converges on to the one hope, on to an objective whose value is known.

Bachelard.

Easter was approaching and the local Catholic church had asked Paddy Roe to relight the candles of the church with fire made with Aboriginal firesticks. This rekindling of the candles which otherwise burn the whole year symbolises for the Catholics the resurrection of the body of Christ. The church made this request of Paddy Roe in a spirit of cooperation and with a profound respect for Aboriginal culture; this culture was called upon to participate in church ritual at its most holy moment. This was not just a question of lighting a little fire, the moment was imbued with a whole cultural politics, by which I mean the way in which the symbols of one culture are arrayed against the symbols of another.

Let us examine this situation first from the White side, then from the Aboriginal side. For European cultures, fire has a rich range of associations which go beyond the confines of its religious use. It is sexuality and love (the 'flame' of passion), it is 'enlightenment', it is the spirit which rises heavenwards in old rituals like cremation and it 'endures'

179

as in the Olympic Games torch. It is the central symbol for the home (the 'hearth') with all the suggestions of comfort and warmth that this brings. Similarly it is the magic which transforms natural things into cultural things; it turns raw things into food, and thus accompanies the most basic of social rituals, the dinner.

When we sit in comfort and look into the fire, our eyes glaze over in a funny way and we dream. Perhaps the primeval nature of the fire closes our mouths and opens our minds onto our unconscious desires. If we manage to express these reveries, they might take the form of a poem (or a song). For instance, Paul Eluard:

> *In the bright crystal of your eyes*
> *Show the havoc of fire, show its inspired works*
> *And the paradise of its ashes.*

Perhaps one of the Catholics was in a similar state of reverie when he thought about the Easter rituals for 1983. He might have imagined himself pulling a box of Redheads out of his pocket to relight a candle in the vestry, which he would afterwards accept from a choirboy to relight the candle during mass with suitable solemnity. How much more appropriate he might have thought, to have an original source of fire, from the very country itself, fire made in a way which is as old as the Aboriginal inhabitants of the land: an autochthonous source of fire. Fire without history will beget a resurrection without history, a resurrection as old as the act of fire-making.

It is always good for the church to reconstruct a permanence for itself when it lands in foreign places, to adapt to its surroundings and bring their strangeness within its fold, to be reasonable and accepting until the strange things are totally assimilated by that fold of understanding which is the maternal and feminine part of the church, the church which is otherwise dominated by that one exclusive symbol of the cross.

Furthermore, there are Aboriginal people in the congregation, and a gesture must be made towards the culture which they have largely left behind. We are in the era of multiculturalist politics, not assimilation. Let the two fires burn side by side, or rather, let the 'first' fire give of its light, its life, its seed for the sake of the church, and then quietly retreat. Paddy Roe must be asked if he will do this for the church, since he is a kind of priest for the Aboriginal people.

Paddy Roe is sitting under his old tamarind tree dreaming about travelling. He has to go to get the wood to make his *ilbi*, firesticks. Krim, Ray Keogh and myself are recruited to the task. 'I come too!' announces Butcher Joe, beaming, with his hat on, and we head out towards *Garrigarrigabu.*

The firesticks are cut from very dry, light dead wood. A piece about five centimetres in diameter and sixty centimetres long is split at one end. Placed on the ground, a wedge already prepared is driven through the split into the ground and this secures that end while opening a centimetre gap. Later someone will hold down the other end while the fire-maker works. The handpiece is made from the same wood, but is whittled down until it is like a sheath-knife. The gap in the other piece of wood is then filled with grass and dried kangaroo dung. The handpiece is held firmly in both hands and its edge is rubbed across the split in the wood. As one works firmly and regularly at first, two darkened grooves appear and hot warm dust starts to fall on the tinder. In accelerating after two or three minutes, this tinder is supposed to catch, and one blows on it to give the flame life. But it wouldn't work. Paddy Roe said that the wood was too wet, and Butcher Joe complained that he didn't have the 'wind'. We young fellas didn't have the right technique or weren't fit enough either. I suggested to Paddy Roe that we try a spot of gunpowder or some ground-up match head. No gunpowder and the match head didn't work either. Had this attempt at *bricolage* been successful, we might have had to warn the Catholics that the 'purity' of the symbolic exchange had been disrupted: the Redheads had reappeared. After all, fire is also a symbol of purification.

Our attempts at making fire were, in the long run, unsuccessful (we needed to be hungry and have a fat goanna waiting to be cooked). Most often we would all burst into laughter as the person sweating away at the task ran out of 'wind'. Something which was once necessary for survival transferred across cultures to be re-read as a source of amusement. Then all this work on the *ilbi* had another cultural consequence. It helped produce a text which joins in the spirit of the initial quotation from Bachelard. On one of the following days Paddy Roe came to us with his *ilbi*, a story and a song.

This was a man -
in *bugarrigarra* he bin walkin' 'round you know -
an' he had his grandsons -
grandsons with 'im -

So they wanted to cook something -
'Ah, we'll have to get-im *ilbi*,'[87] he say - -
'We'll have to get *ilbi* - - -
aaah we want to cook these, lizard you know - -
yalgi anything' –

'All right,' he say -
so old man went 'round he get the wood -
that stick -
cut-im -
he musta cut-im with I dunno what -
might be stone tommyhawk -
or might be -
I dunno what he had anyway -

So he bring back that stick -
so he start now he wanta make a fire - -
you see -
an' these lil-lil' fellas all singing out -
because he's a *gamirda* -
gamirda -
gamirda is, ah, grandfather
Stephen: Ah
Gamirda is the grandfather -
'All right grandfather you better make *ilbi*,' they say -
'*walarrguna ilbi gamirda*' -

So when the oldfella start -
this one, you know -
he start -

182

an' lil-lil' fellas all sing now -
(Sings with a jerky rhythm and developing crescendo.)

> *Ilbi walarrgun djinar*
> *gamirda gulbidan bidan*
> *ilbi walarrgun djinar*
> *gamirda gulbidan bidan*
> *ilbi walarrgun djinar*
> *gamirda gulbidan bidan*
> *ilbi walarrgun djinar*
> *gamirda gul ...*[88]

(Laughter.)
Ilbi is, that one (Taps sticks)   *walarrgun djinar,* this one *walarrgun*
(Rubs sticks).
Stephen: Moving mm, walarrgun.
Djinar, ilbi walarrgun, djinar   moving, this one   *gamirda,*
grandfather   *gulbidan bidan,* that's his name   *gamirda gulbidan*
bidan   he say you   know *gamirda gulbidan bidan.*
(Sings with even more emphasis.)

> *Ilbi walarrgun djinar*
> *gamirda gulbidan bidan*
> *ilbi walarrgun djinar*
> *gamirda gulbidan bidan*
> *ilbi walarrgun djinar*
> *gamirda gulbidan bidan ...*

(Laughter.)
Make big fire now, they cooking.

Lizard Story

Now these people all come from, desert[89] -
before they come to that Looma[90] -
they come from desert -
aah - - - -

When they come from - -
because them people - -
wanted to run away -
the country was too hot for them in desert -
they wanted to come back to river country -
to live -
eer - - - -

So mother said to these fellas - -
I take youfellas back to river - -
cool country -
hot country we must leave that place -

now dis lot all -
this lot all *nalyag*[91] -
well they're not *nalyag*, I mean - -
these people bin all *djalubardju*[92] -
djalubardju? -
all *djalubardju* -
this lot -
in that *bugarrigarra* -
bugarrigarra, dreamtime you know *bugarrigarra* -

So -
when mother was walkin' front, them little fella comin' behind all the
time -
all right this little fellas singing -

184

behind -
mother lookin' for something, you know he want to get in the road for eat -
this little fella all the time singing -

djalubardju ngayu
djalubardju ngayu

bani wiya wiya
bani wiya wiya

djalubardju ngayu
djalubardju ngayu

bani wiya wiya [93]

He look back -
hello one brother dead (Turns one wooden lizard on his back) -
oh, he look -
oh, he tell mother -
oh *warndjarri mambardu gud* -
tjuwa (...) yarranj gud njiyama -
he tell-im 'You can die, I go with 'nother brother' -
So he off again -

djalubardju ngayu
djalubardju ngayu

bani wiya wiya
bani wiya wiya

djalubardju ngayu
djalubardju ngayu

bani wiya wiya

He look back again -
hello 'nother sister die (Turns lizard over, laugh) -
ah you can die, I got with one brother -
he leave-im all dead, finish, people -

djalubardju ngayu
djalubardju ngayu

bani wiya wiya
bani wiya wiya

djalubardju ngayu
djalubardju ngayu

bani wiya wiya

He look back again -
hello 'nother one dead -
aah -
he said -
'You can die,' last one he tell-im, 'I go with mummy' -

djalubardju ngayu
djalubardju ngayu

bani wiya wiya

(Breaks off) He never sing, he never sing -
last one bin there -
no this is in the river -
river is here you know -
that's the river -
oh that river is too big -
the little fella can't swim -
'All right,' he say, 'Come on,' he tell-im -
mother never take any notice only this fella taking notice -

186

oh mother seen-em too but this is the one that's singing -
'All right you jump on my back,' he tell-im, 'baby' -
I swim across with yupella -

He swim across with 'im -
he swim across with 'im right over other side -
when he get other side he jump down -

> *djalubardju ngayu*
> *djalubardju ngayu*

> *bani wiya wiya*
> *bani wiya wiya*

> *djalubardju ngayu*
> *djalubardju ngayu*

> *bani wiya wiya*

Hello his mummy is dead (Acts out turning lizard over, laughs) -
he's only one left - -
'Oh yupella all can die' he tell-em -
'mummy brothers sisters -
I just stop by meself' -

> *djalubardju ngayu*
> *djalubardju ngayu*

> *bani wiya wiya*
> *bani wiya wiya*

> *djalubardju ngayu*
> *djalubardju ngayu*

> *bani wiya wiya*

He's dead too (Laugh) -
finish -
(Soft, breathy voice) all dead every one -
but they all turn into lizard now (Laugh)
Krim: Aah
All turn into lizard they bin human being comin' up -
this is only one little boy had the sense -
what he singing -
not these people -
he only know -

Because they can't live in this country as human being - -
they'll have to, live like a lizard so people can eat them -
(Laugh)

Stephen: Other side of river
Eh?
Stephen: When they get to the other side of the river
When they get other side of the river now they all live in the river country now -
all over here in cold country -
but not in the desert -
oh might be in desert, but other, other -
lizard -
but they live here -

And that's only little boy had sense - -
youngest brother -
that's that *djalubardju* -
all this lot *djalubardju*

INTELLECTUALS, POWER AND TRUTH

You people try and dig little bit more deep -
you bin digging only white soil -
try and find the black soil inside ...
                                        Paddy Roe.

These people used to eat themselves too, they used to kill one another.
Stephen: Oh yeah.
Eat himself, anything   just like animals bin eatin' themself too   you
know.
Stephen: Not those djalubardju?
Yeah *djalubardju.*
Stephen: Used to eat themselves?
Oh might be some people used to eat them.
Stephen: Ooh.
Well just like eeer tiger want to eat pussycat er whatname? kangaroo,
kangaroo want to eat that grass (Laugh) mm it's a thing like that   or
anything you know eer dingo want to kill that, kangaroo   but we want
to kill that kangaroo we want to eat him (Laugh) it's a thing like that.
Stephen: What, people used to eat people?
Before   before   we don't know.
Stephen: When they're dead.
I mean   well ah   they kill themself for eat   that's why they used to
run away, everywhere.
Stephen: Oh.
For eat   well eer I s'pose eer these things *marrala* and all these
fellas you know we don't know what sorta eer people they been   in
bugarrigarra   they musta bin eatin' somebody too.
Stephen: In bugarrigarra.
In *bugarrigarra.*
Stephen: But not in real life.
No no no not in real life   this is all *bugarrigarra*   in dreamtime we

189

don't know what was (Laugh)   'cos that's why they mighta run away
too   we wouldn't know really because eer   well I s'pose we didn't
have much time   with our old people   Butcher Joe's old people
fathers and all them people they mighta   they mighta forgettin' things
too   coming this way more how these things bin happening you
know   eer well just like we people we only got little bit in our mind
too today   we musta lost lotta things too (Laugh)   that's why   we
like to save something this time   while we living   there won't be any
more o' these things once we gone (Laugh)   that's right?
Stephen: Well you can …
'Cos nobody got-em   'cos my people haven't got-em too   already,
down Looma might be big big places might be La Grange big big places
might be One Arm Point big big places nobody got-em (Laugh)
these only things, ah well   I didn't really think about these things, I
had all these things in my mind too but then old Butcher Joe started all
these things hee, he wake me up a bit (Laugh) because I know the game
too you know?
Stephen: Mm, I wonder what made him think, that he must do this.
Weell, he first started in the whatname   in Beagle Bay Mission
might be Catholic priest mighta eeer …
Krim: Yeah, Father Francis.
Ask-im for all these sorta things (Laugh) you know eer …
Krim: And Mary Durack too.
Yeah   to do these books and things   'cos Father Francis worked with
him, he musta think about   might be this kind, you know (Gestures
money, laughter).
Stephen: Yeah.
Yeah   mm.

I remember one time he come up here, you seee   well   I dunno
whether he took notice about this old fella or, anyway he told him the
story and that, he made a book   you know   all these things he write
everything down for him and er eer   'cos he's one of the man got
bugarrigarra too you know, that priest   and that church, you call it,
that's *bugarrigarra* too (Laugh).
Krim: Their bugarrigarra (Laugh).
Eh? That's right?
Stephen: Mm … Christian?
That's only *bugarrigarra* because nobody never seen true person
(Laughter)   you know, I don't think, did they?   did they ever see
anything, true person?
Stephen: For this man, for Christian?
Well I mean, yeah.

Stephen: Yeah.
Krim: They have seen sometime.
Stephen: Oh, yeah, used to live.
Eh?
Stephen: God.
God.
Stephen: Yeah, came to Earth.
Krim: His son.
Stephen: As his son.
Yeah, yeah.
Stephen: He sent his son down.
Yeah, well.
Stephen: And everybody killed him, and so ever since then we gotta feel very sorry (Laughter).
He had father? He had father?
Stephen: That's real God, yeah.
Eh?
Stephen: God.
Yeah but did they see God?
Stephen: Nuh, never.
Well that's it.
Stephen: Yeah.
That's the start of it now   I know Jesus was a human being, then he gone   but his father; nobody don't know nobody never see-im because he's a *bugarrigarra.*
Stephen: That's right.
He come out (Laugh).
Stephen: That's right.
Yeah   Oh I can't with these   somebody when I tell them you know? 'Oh no no no'   'Yes but, Who's he? Jesus' father?'   you know   must be *bugarrigarra.*
Stephen: It's like a power.
Yeah power.
Stephen: You can't see it, might be everywhere —that's what they say these days.
Yeah.
Stephen: Oh sometimes they used to make pictures of him, old man, white beard.
Yeah.
Stephen: But everybody say, 'Oh no that's wrong', really you don't know what he look like.
No, that's right   well I dunno what these look like too but I only seen the lizard today (Laughter)   that's why I made these (Picks up wooden

lizards) but when he was *djalubardju* I dunno what sorta animal or human being he was   mm   but that's *bugarrigarra* today now this is all *bugarrigarra* yunmi talking, we never seen that human being   just like I said about this whatname   the monster   One Arm   (Laugh) not One Arm, lighthouse.
Stephen: Yeah.
Lighthouse? Well that's *marrala* bin walkin' there, that's his track.
Stephen: Marrala?
Marrala, yeah he's a man he bin singing   but that's his track   (Laugh).
Stephen: Where did he go, from there?
Right inside the sea.
Stephen: He come out from there?
(Sigh.) He mighta go somewhere else from there I think.
Stephen: That's where he finished up.
Er, not really   I think he musta just went in there from shame   'cos first time he meet all the woman, mother-in-law and all these sorta things   that's why we got mother-in-LAW today, from *bugarrigarra* he got daughter   well that daughter is mine   he might be promise me you know.
Krim: Mm.
So I gotta feed that mother tucker anything, plenty this way and bit of everything you know   'til the baby grow big, little bit   I take-im 'way, might be that high   then I grow him up you know 'til he get woman   time's when woman, 'Oh that's right, that's woman' we see, you know, 'Ah' then he come to be woman then   but just like I take little boy everywhere see   you know, er it's like that   oh not really, but old people you know, he take-em   it's like that ah English say, 'What that?' 'That's my wife' (Incredulous) 'WHAT?' (Laughter) 'Yeah' 'You should be in jail' but that man know what he's doin' (Laugh) he's not silly   he know he   he know   he know how big he gonta be before he come to woman   but he can feed him take him everywhere whatever he likes   and nothing happen (Laugh) he got too much this one too (Gesture 'brains', laugh)   but he grow him up then that two he come, never leave one another   'til they die, same thing or man die first, woman'll have to find 'nother man   but if woman die then he'll have to find 'nother woman, if he want to   woman too same if his man die if he want 'nother man he can find him but if nothing, no   (Soft) you see today marriage in church, ooh big, everything you know   tomorrow, one week time, 'Where's that man gone?' he's with 'nother woman somewhere now (Laughter) you see? very shame, he fool his church, you know   but that's the black man's law, that way now, I say you know he know   'cos ...

I remember one time -
one bloke went in jail for seven years -
because eer the girl was twelve year old -
but that's his promised girl (Laugh) you see?
Krim: Mm.
Yeah, that's his promised girl -

Now I come back, I dunno too -
I bin working out in Roebuck Plain country -
in the windmills -
I told you 'bout that cyclone come, not very long -

So when I come back I hear that man in jail -
'What's wrong with 'im?'
'Oh well, they took the girl away, put-im back in the convent -
and put the man in for seven years' -
'Yeah, what wrong?' I said to welfare -
welfare, they bring me there -

'No no no,' I said -
'That's his promised GIRL -
that's his PROMISED girl -
he married about that high (Laugh) -
he can carry his wife -
anyway where he travel around if he can't walk (Laughter) -
if he get tired -
you know, 'til he grow big -
when he grow big, he know, he got this one,' I said (Laugh) -
you know -
when he grow big, then he see, he's a woman -

THEN he know what to do -
make a woman out of him -

But he can walk around for years and years just like that -
nothing else -
oh I got mad too -
'You people try and dig little bit more deep -
you bin digging only white soil -
try and find the black soil inside' (Laughter) -
YEAH -
I said to him -

'So what are we gonta do about it?'
'Well he should be out -
he shouldn't be inside, where his woman?' -
'Oh, in convent'
'Well that's not right (Laugh) -
you only put-im in white man's law what about this law? (Laugh) -
this, girl is given to his er son-in-law -
mother-in-law give him -
he's married, finish -
when they grow up they're our people -
never leave one another -
from the day they join up -
one gotta die' -
that's true too -
(Soft) but er - -

Oh they get-im out -
they got-im out again they let-im go -
that man, 'You look after 'im'
'Oh I will too,' I tell-im -

So he come out -
he come outa the jail -
they went 'nother court, not, er well er musta been whatname - -
well they said *prole* something is it?

Krim: Parole, yeah, parole.
Parole, yeah.
Stephen: Well he didn't do anything anyway.

Eh?
Stephen: He didn't do anything.
Well he didn't do anything -
they let him out -
but if anything wrong again between that time and anything well that's
nothing - -
nothing -
er, they put-im back again -

But he know that man know they give-im his girl back too we got-im
outa the convent (Laughter) -
give-im back again -
in La Grange -

194

we bring-im back again from La Grange, they had 'im there in convent -
and man there in Broome jail (Laugh) -
so we got-im back, it's finished -
so he bin stop now today tupella live together now no worries (Laugh) -
his time was over

Paddy Roe is in his culture what Europeans might call an 'intellectual' in theirs. This does not *necessarily* mean that he is endowed with a profound or wide-ranging knowledge. Rather, it can be taken to mean that he operates as an agent for a particular Aboriginal institution: traditional culture of the Broome area. This definition of intellectuals points to the *specific* functioning of their work rather than their 'general' knowledge; rather than being cumulative or encyclopedic, knowledges come into play in specific encounters, often between institutions, they work in specific sites and govern the plausibility of the statements produced there so that what is said can count as being 'the truth' for a certain time.

From the discussion with Paddy Roe, and his story, it is easy to see how different cultures produce different sorts of truths which hold good only within their own systems. But Paddy Roe's approach is 'intellectual' in the sense that he doesn't dismiss the white man's institutions out of hand; he reads them from a perspective which takes into account cultural similarity and difference. Christianity and *bugarrigarra* thus have 'invisibility' in common.

The intellectual is on the margins of the common body of knowledge. By knowing things which come from elsewhere (the 'frontiers' of science and technology, the strange, almost perverse discourses of the humanities, and other cultures) he or she makes raids on common myths at the same time as building up new ones which will come to count as common knowledge one day. It is Paddy Roe's confidence in the knowledge of his own culture which enables him to challenge in such a forceful way European notions of marriage, and he saves one of his countrymen from seven years of suffering. This is perhaps the power of the intellectual; to intervene in a situation and tell a story which can change the conventions for understanding things.

Michel Foucault was a French philosopher who has intervened in ways similar to Paddy Roe. He acted to set up a Prisoners' Information Group in Paris, and while working in this specific context he asked questions about the role of intellectuals in society, about the part they are supposed to play in the production of 'truth':

> ... *truth isn't outside power, or lacking in power: contrary to a myth which would repay further study, truth isn't the reward of free spirits, the child of protracted solitude, nor the priv-*

ilege of those who have succeeded in liberating themselves.
Truth is a thing of this world: it is produced only by virtue of
multiple forms of constraint. And it induces regular effects of
power. Each society has its regimes of truth, its 'general pol-
itics' of truth: that is, the types of discourse which it accepts
and makes function as true; the mechanisms and instances
which enable one to distinguish true and false statements, the
means by which each is sanctioned; the techniques and proce-
dures accorded value in the acquisition of truth; the status of
those who are charged with saying what counts as true.[94]

There are two small 'myths' circulating about the purveyors of truth
and power in our society. One is that all politicians are liars, the other
is that intellectuals are ineffective, cut off from the 'real world'. Using
work like Foucault's we can work to dispel these myths, or at least point
to whatever makes such statements possible at all.

The statement about politicians being liars indicates not so much that
they are evil, but that they are strategists of plausibility or truth—not of
universal truths, which don't exist, but of transitory statements, words
which have a particular effect within specific sectors. The plausibility
of their statements is connected precisely to their *knowledge* of situa-
tional tactics, they are not dealing in 'dirty' power which is divorced
from regimes of truth. Their ministries are constantly engaged in the
production of knowledges to which the politicians have specialised access. They are not, therefore, acting blindly, seduced by a lust for power
which would sweep aside all considerations of truth. Truth and power
are coproductive.

And if the intellectual is seen by the politician as being some sort
of threat, then it is precisely because the intellectual can make use of a
number of techniques to question the plausibility of the politician's statements as instances of truth-production. Intellectuals only have the power to do this because of *their* institutions: their régimes of truth, their
multiple connections with other institutions (the judiciary, hospitals, ar-
mament research and cultural production). The universities and colleges
are powerful to the extent that they play specific roles in these areas.
But they are saved from the responsibility for power by the notion of the
ivory tower. It is imagined that truth emerges in quiet contemplation or
experiment and that once it is written down it has a universal value. But
it is clear that the words of intellectuals are subject to similar constraints
to those of politicians. A régime of truth conditions their production and
their eventual distribution to the places where they count, where they
have some effect of power.

Intellectuals are not operating in universal knowledge with a universal method. They are strategists who take sides in debates and struggles.

They are not *only* thinkers, and silence is certainly not the material on which they work. They are producers of stories, and stories can have very powerful effects.

Ngurralala lawurrga-ngana gandji
PLACE ——————— bone

warramba lirrin ganganayi-yana
dance   white paint   he has

Daman

1983, 76.5 cm x 57 cm, gouache and pastel on D'Arches paper

DAMAN (WARFARE)

Yeah - - - -
yeah - - - -
this is about old *Walmadanj*
Stephen: That's his name.
That's his name *Walmadanjburu* -

That, er -
other side of Barred Creek -
waterhole -
in Price Point -
that's *Walmadanj* -

I dunno what happened really they musta, these people up here (Draws
    in the sand) musta kill his mother -
eeer might be in the tribal fight or something like that you know they
had -
they musta kill his mother - - - - -

Ah - -
might be accident you know
Stephen: Yeah.
In the fight -

So this old fella -
when he bin grow up -
so he know his mother got killed this side, you know (Laugh) -
so - - - - -

So they went from here -
straight across - -
they camp might be two or three nights in the, road -
in the bush you know 'til they reach that place Dampier Down -

Then they seen the -
just about sundown they can see fire and everything you know -
'Oh must be big mob of people fire everywhere' -

So they wait 'til proper dark -
just about midnight you know everybody proper sound asleep -

So they aaall come in here walk around that camp nobody get up - -
nobody get up aall dead sleep -
so they kill-im whole lot with spear (Laugh) -
last ones might be some bin singin' out you know they just leave the
    spear with 'im (Laugh) -
right through here you see (Laugh) -
heart -
leave-im there -

Some mighta got away 'cos they didn't have 'nuff spears too
Krim: Mm.
To kill all you know (Laugh) -

Soo -
and in this *Wandurnanj* -
Wandurnanj -
Irninginj here very close together -
but *Wandurnanj-*

Wandurnanj -
this is my people camp here again -
Nygina people -
all mix Yawur, Nyigina, Garadjeri this one in *Wandurnanj* -
that's sheep camp country sheep station -

And this one - -
all Djaberdjaber people -
Walmadanj - - -
when they come back from Dampier Down after they kill all them people -
they come back through here -
right up to *Wandurnanj* -

Everybody sleep too middle night they come through -
oh they just walk 'round here and walk back to their country -
Walmadanj -

you know (Laugh) - -

That's coming back from Dampier Down -
and these people here - - -
they bin walk from here, before they went 'nother way, they went 'round
    this way -
they couldn't find their track they find-im coming back-track -

So they look around for track next morning these people, 'Who bin kill
    these people?' -
'Ooh here their track, gone' -

They track-em up now -
they want to kill them people too -
they track-em up right up here they come here oooh just about dark oooh
    they can see fire and everything you know -
everywhere -
'Oh here they are -
here they are' they said these people -

So this lot got nothing to do [with it] (Laugh) -
they're not trouble people -

All right -
night-time they come they kill all these fellas -
(Laugh)
Krim: They didn't do anything.
Eh? They didn't do anything they all come back finish -
that's the people got killed
Stephen: Oh yeah
For nothing - -
he very cunning that old fella - -
(Laugh)

So Yawur people, Nyigina people, Garadjeri people -
all got killed everybody here all mixed -
and this lot all Nyigina people too -
Garadjeri people this lot too -
Garadjeri Nyigina -
might be little bit Mangala
Stephen: They might have killed their own people.
Eh? well they kill their own people, yeah (Laugh) -
that's their countrymen (Laugh) -
they thought these fellas bin kill these fellas

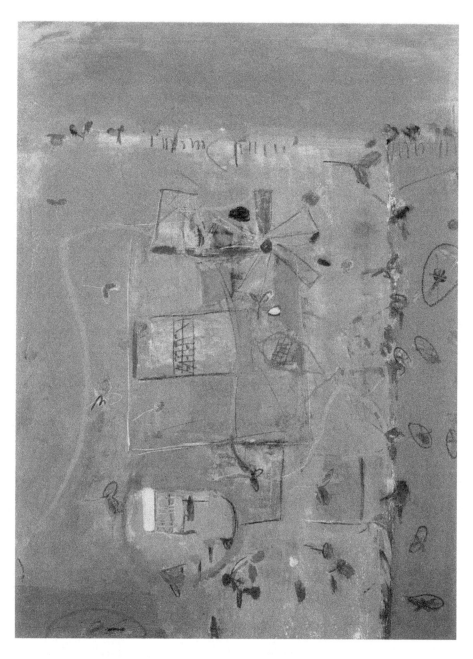

Ligne de Fuite
1983, 76 cm x 57 cm, gouache and pastel on D'Arches paper

Lawurrunbadjar imana-yana mandjarra
Red-belly snake   went   ————

bulbulindina-yana
searching/digging

The Disappearance of Anthropology

Ethnology almost met a paradoxical death that day in 1971 when the Filipino government decided to return the few dozen Tasaday recently discovered deep in the jungle, where they had lived for eight centuries undisturbed by the rest of mankind, to their primitive state, out of reach of colonists, tourists and ethnologists. This was at the initiative of the anthropologists themselves, who saw the natives decompose immediately on contact, like a mummy in the open air. For ethnology to live, its object must die. But the latter revenges itself by dying for having been 'discovered', and defies by its death the science that wants to take hold of it.

Baudrillard.

One thing in any case is certain; man is neither the oldest nor the most constant problem that has been posed for human knowledge.

Foucault.

'Ligne de Fuite' (page 203) is Krim's most radical statement, not so much in terms of what it sees in the country, but in how it unites the themes of his landscapes and at the same time blows apart the conventions of the genre. With its two horizons, our whole sense of verticality and horizontality is thrown into question. In some respects it looks like any of the other paintings with the same space for the sky at the top of the canvas. But the second 'horizon' falling away from this one makes us want to turn the canvas so that there is a second painting. This is perfectly possible. But this possibility does something to the area of canvas representing the country. From what perspective are we now viewing it? We are no longer looking from a high angle, but from directly above: an

205

aerial view. Large light blue traces traversing this area confirm this effect since they look very much like Paddy Roe's sand drawings. Windmills, trees, springs and paddocks combine in this section of the canvas to create what is more like an abstract representation of Roebuck Plains.

The vertical horizon on the right of the canvas, the long deep-blue rectangle, does more than just double the top horizon. It 'gives depth' in the same sense that Paddy Roe communicates a sense of unending depth to the water supplies which lie under the country. This area merges with the 'country' as a number of motifs drift across from that area to take up residence within it. Thus, in a quite conventional way, the separation of sky and country is maintained by defining the 'other' blue area as water. But is it? What if those motifs were stars?

Within a discipline like Australian landscape painting—a discipline because it has its institutions, with teachers, laws, judges and guardians—advances can only be made within an awareness of the regulations; advances which involve 'flying away' from the conventions of the genre at the same time as setting up other ways of seeing things.

This same process applies to science, since as it slowly transforms, the things it takes most for granted suddenly become visible from another perspective and no longer occupy central positions. The analysis of anthropology as a *discourse,* one which emanates from tertiary institutions of education, shows it to be positioned relative to other discourses. *It* discusses Aborigines and *Aborigines* discuss Aborigines, but only anthropology has the monopoly on 'truth', the 'true' way of discussing Aboriginal affairs as far as other powerful institutions are concerned. The law, for instance, always calls upon anthropological testimony in land rights cases.

It also joins forces with humanism to the extent that it takes the category of 'Man' as central and necessary to its reasoning. It is important to study human societies, it says tautologically, because we are all human: it is important to know about ourselves, and we can do this best by comparing and contrasting the Others. Then we might find out what is common, universal or 'deep down'. Differences are therefore never irreducible, since under the *one* sign of Man sameness will always be discovered.

Anthropology is a curious discipline, one which is in a state of crisis, both in Australia and overseas. This crisis takes a number of forms, traversing the theory of the discipline, the practices of its field workers, the shape of the texts it produces, and the relationship with the people who are supposedly its objects of study. It maintains a position of power over these people through the ritual of the communicative event. This is a ritual which it shares with psychoanalysis; the two disciplines are bedfellows[95] (strange as it may seem) because their typical communicative event is one in which they put their subjects in a situation of 'double bind': they both require their subjects, in the fieldwork situation or on the couch, to *keep talking* and at the same time to 'remain quiet'.

The professional's knowledge depends on listening to, and interpreting the words of the unknown subjects, but these words are at the same time disarmed. What is actually said by the subjects is lost as it gives away to the more powerful discourse which interprets the words and finds a 'deeper meaning' for them. Anthropology discovers *social structures* in this process, and psychoanalysis discovers the *structures of the unconscious*.

Both these knowledges work on the individual subject for the most part; they are constructed on the basis of files, dossiers and notes on individuals: 'case studies'. This 'individualising' has one offshoot at least; the political formation of these individuals tends to be ignored. When one is trying to find out about social structures or structures of the unconscious as relatively stable things, it is best to skirt around the potentially disruptive area of political understandings, especially since political questioning tends to involve the people asking the questions. The way they pose the questions positions them politically.

The same thing works from the other direction. If the subject being questioned starts to break the envelope of silence and impotence which surrounds the interview by calling for his or her comrades and pointing out that they have a common struggle, then the power difference on which the interview situation was set up begins to crumble. This

The origin of table manners? A Parisian moment when Robert Brandhof flew in from France

is precisely what happened in Australia in the seventies. The political unification of Aboriginal peoples in their struggle for better living conditions, land rights and political representation gave them a common discourse which rejected the activity of authoritarian investigation of their societies, whether this was supposedly in terms of knowledge (anthropology) or welfare (missions and government departments).

Since then, anthropology has fragmented and reformed. It is less likely to pronounce on a whole civilisation, or even tribe. It has gone underground to a certain extent and is now less recognisable. The new anthropologists are dispassionate operators in the bureaucratic encounter between Aboriginal communities, the government and mining companies. These new professionals work for mining companies investigating Aboriginal communities so that conflict over sacred sites can be avoided. (These sites have to be identified so that mining companies will not desecrate them when they start digging or drilling.)

Sometimes these new anthropologists work for Aboriginal Land Councils, but they are generally politically ineffective, and this is one of the conditions for the successful image of the 'objective' social scientist. They wield a discourse which counts as 'true' in a field which is without doubt politically charged in more than one sense: mining companies encounter opposition from anti-nuclear groups, Aboriginal land rights groups, conservationists and anti-multinational groups.

One particular scientific philosophy which shapes the anthropological texts and governs the strategies of works in the field, is *empiricism,* a knowledge which produces itself through observation and experiment. This exact and meticulous scientific method derives from the natural sciences like physics and botany and became the basis for the human sciences less than two centuries ago. The study of 'man' is no older than that.

The analysis of people by other people requires specific techniques. It starts with observation. Techniques of counting, measuring and classifying produce what is known as *data* or *facts* under conditions such as the isolation of individual subjects which we already noted. We are all familiar with techniques such as the questionnaire for obtaining 'facts' about society. And we are very familiar with the form in which these results appear in the daily papers: 'Surveys show 25% of the population attends church services ...' or '85% more blacks than whites are in prison'. The appeal to statistics constitutes one of the authoritative effects of this discourse—a link with the 'purity' of mathematics.

But, as many other accounts opposed to this kind of knowledge have shown, empirical research is fraught with difficulty, not the least of which is its dependence on the cooperation and confidence of the subjects from which it requires a verbal or written response to its enquiries.

In a situation already loaded in favour of the 'science', surely the person being interviewed will give the response that they think should be given in that situation.

Let us go back to the birth of anthropology, a discipline which grew with, and was made possible by, European imperialism. Not only did it participate in colonial expansion, performing both a fact-finding and a tutelary role in relation to the colonised peoples, but the rise of the study of Man corresponded to the dwindling of the study of God. Man turned away from his deity only to find his own image. This was to become the basis for knowledge in the nineteenth and twentieth centuries, such that today it seems quite normal for us to keep trying to find out more and more about ourselves, as if Man were the focal point of the quest for Truth.

Anthropology contributed to the construction of this universal entity, Man, in a paradoxical manner: anthropology denounces ethnocentrism in its quest for the universal nature of man by saying that all men are equal.[96] But at the same time, it can only be a *European* science (therefore ethnocentric) because of the conditions of its birth, and it constructs the face of universal man by repeatedly comparing European man's image to that of 'the Others'—the tribal or pre-industrial peoples whose societies are seen symbolically as the unconscious counterpart to modern western man's consciousness of himself as a labouring, investigating, suffering being—one who has lost 'nature' and innocence with rise of industrialisation.

While the human sciences look out and away towards other shores to feed this insatiable desire that the central concept of Man seems to have for new information, different information about itself, psychoanalysis looks inwards to the world of dreams and finds ways to make Man confess. Again, it is the absence of the church which makes this new confessional possible. Secret, unsayable desires now emerge (as if long-repressed) and are shaped into the figures of the discourse of psychoanalysis; *complexes* and *drives* become the internal mechanisms of Man. Psychoanalysis and human sciences like anthropology are like mystic guardians which, armed with rules of interpretation, stand at the borderline between Man and that 'Otherness' (stretching both inwards and outwards) which threatens the concept of man as unitary and knowable.

But even if central concepts like God and Man are displaced, and have to come down from their pedestals, they are borne away on the shoulders of their institutions which bury them under a myriad of practices. Nietzsche announced the death of God, and the church lives on. Michel Foucault announced the death of Man and the human sciences dominate popular conceptions of knowledge. Why is psychology the discipline which is central to the training of primary school teachers? It is as if everything of importance about Man is individual and mental, as if collective acts and statements count for nothing. If we attribute everything to the silent world of the mind, then we stand little chance of contradiction.

But silence is not the condition of the social relations which form us as subjects, it is noise, it is the clash of incompatible discourses. It is in language that Man has always found his definition, not in the mental or 'real' worlds which are supposed to exist beyond it. In language, or rather in the Babel of tongues, people find multiple definitions of self and other, and it is in these relations of difference that conflict and pleasure are articulated, spoken.

After so many years of interrogation, testing, quantification and analysis of man's actions, there must come a realisation that people are, after all, only bodies, and that their minds don't conceal any truths to be revealed on a closer examination.

With the death of Man, a space is opened up in which we can think about the shape and distribution of communicative forms as they regularly appear and disappear. Then there would no longer be a shadow cast over each text that demands that we read it in relation to *any* central concept. Without Man standing over our shoulder, we can finally ask questions about the text. Where is this text speaking from? How does it position me? Under what circumstances was it produced? What rhetorical devices does it employ? Is it likely to lead me where I want to go?

Scholars, and other investigators, can then perhaps loosen the hold they have on individual bodies and content themselves with the quite concrete traces they leave behind. Isn't it a very basic and important thing to know, from someone's tracks, where they have come from and which way they are going? Reading tracks is like reading texts. We know where anthropology came from, and it was once easy to track the anthropological text, but now, with the virtual disappearance of the discipline, these tracks might bear the marks of *any* institution, and it is harder to follow them.

Heliotrope I

1983, 76 cm x 57 cm, acrylic and pastel on D'Arches paper

Painting as Heliotrope

The very opposition of appearing and disappearing, the entire lexicon ... of day and night, of the visible and the invisible, of the present and the absent—all this is possible only under the sun.

Derrida.

Krim's blue series of paintings are *night paintings* and this, I should point out immediately, is only a metaphor.

But perhaps the observer was under the impression of having been led astray, away from Roebuck Plains, and dumped into the deep-water channels of the Indian Ocean? Let's be liberal; of course you were! After a long hot day reading paintings (or living in the Plains) a dip in the ocean—a change to cool blue—is certainly called for.

But what is a heliotrope? It is something which *turns with the sun* or *turns towards the sun* (Greek: *helios*, 'sun'; *tropos*, 'a turn') like a sunflower. It is also the name for a stone: a deep green quartz shot through with blood-red jasper. Aha! The paintings are starting to emerge. But they are paintings which have turned away from the sun and all that it represents. They are the dark side of the Earth, of light and of living. They are paintings which are resting from the hard work of living on the Plains.

But how did they come to be painted? For once, biographical detail is relevant. Krim was asked to give painting lessons in Broome Prison. All of this series emerged spontaneously during the classes. On the first day Krim instructed the prisoners in non-representational technique. He encouraged liberal application of paint, enjoyment of colour, form and texture for their own sake, and so on. He was talking like that and demonstrating on one of his own canvasses. Suddenly he became aware of a silence—one that had perhaps been going on for a long time, since his painting was nearly finished—he looked up and all eyes were *turned towards him.*

212

Krim had become the sun, for a moment, the figure which enlightens the students. He was able to do this because of the way he was eclipsed by his own task. In turning his attention towards his painting he forgot to supervise his students, to instruct and discipline them. It was precisely this *absence* of 'the teacher' in him which drew the prisoners' attention to him and his work. He was the dark sun in a shadowy interior where dark-skinned prisoners worked away silently in their blue singlets.

Outside the sun was scorching down. Krim had turned away from this outside world to become an honorary prisoner of blue for a while. This turning away turned out to be productive and significant. It seems to me that if he had not done the blue series, the reading of Roebuck Plains would have been incomplete, for it is the alternation of the presence and absence of the sun which ultimately conditions life there. Animals and plants can take a cool breather in the night hours. People used to talk, sing and dance around camp fires, those suns-of-the-night; the givers of light and warmth in the night. Spots of blood-red jasper in the green stone.

Strictly speaking, it is all the other paintings that are heliotropic, painted in the *presence* of the sun (following it around), while the present series of night paintings would be anti-heliotropic. They are conditioned by the *absence* of the sun. It takes an awareness of this absence to bring to light the presence of the sun in the other ones. Strange paradox that the dark painting can be illuminating.

But what also conditions the production of the night series is the virtual absence of the usual motifs: fences, tracks, springs, windmills. They are present as traces, obscured by the dark. We are deprived of our usual support structure, like prisoners, and must seek our consolation in those minimal necessities for painting: colour, form, texture, movement. Will a fence or a windmill ever look the same again when we are once more 'on the outside', in the world of representation? This reduction to basic necessities makes the paintings in the blue series more abstract than most of the others, but they also stand in opposition to them, like painting itself does to the 'reality' it is supposed to represent. This is how this series becomes a metaphor for the night, for that aspect of Roebuck Plains in which things are obscure or not seen properly.

In the night, vague outlines metamorphose into strange objects belonging more to our unconscious dreams than to the country itself. This metamorphosis happens with any painting representing things. The blue series can thus be constructed as metaphorical for the act of painting— transforming things into the world of paint. One of the conditions for painting is that things are not represented (seen or read) *properly* (just as a metaphor like 'the twilight of his years' uses words *figuratively* rather than 'properly' to represent another meaning: old age).

To reiterate: the night series is anti-heliotropic, it is turned away from the sun under which things are seen 'properly'. The night series is therefore figurative, and figuration is what painting is all about.

But the metaphor can be developed further. The organ of perception most important to creating and viewing paintings is the eye. It is the act of seeing which produces the effects of painting; to paint or appreciate painting, the eye must be *turned towards* the image. The centrality of the eye to painting is like the centrality of the sun in the world of stark reality. The similarity of these two orbs—the sun and the eye—has often been noted by the poets.

Shelley, for instance, in his famous last poem 'The Triumph of Life' imagined the sun 'seeing' its own light sent back from a green well, the surface of which acted like a mirror, and was shaped like an eye:

... the sun's image radiantly intense
Burned on the waters of the well that glowed
Like gold ...

As an image, the sun can now take shape, rather than being the white nothingness of a blaze of light (the blank canvas). A world without form becomes shot through with traces of rainbows, fragments of colour as the eye turns from the sun itself to the sun-as-eye. We can now inhabit the landscape created since perception has created the tracks, the figures we know how to read. The sun, says Shelley:

threaded all the forest maze
With winding paths of emerald fire ...[97]

Again we have the image of the heliotrope, and the opposition of water and fire, night and day. It is clear to us now that the paintings create their meaning through a turning away from the blinding radiance of the sun. This must be a constant movement, like the Earth around the sun, since once one figure is established in landscape painting, one 'turn of phrase' as it were, then what the new painting must do is turn away again in order to create. Painting is the act of figurative displacement, dancing away from whatever is 'there'. Painting a landscape is not to 'pin down' its essence, to make it still, but to trace a path which the eye can follow into the space which is tomorrow's painting.

Heliotrope II
1983, 76.5cm x 57 cm, acrylic and pastel on D'Arches paper

THE GOOD OIL COMPANY AND
THE BAD OIL COMPANY

Stephen: What was that one again, that story?
Cloud?
Stephen: From Dampier Downs.[98]
Oh that one, I seen that one, yeah.

Oh this is some oil people went through -
in Dampier Down country -
Dampier Down country -

But that's our country too, Nyigina country proper that's where my uncles
    come from my mother's, relations, proper -
Nyigina people -
and father too -
old full-blood father and mother, you know -
that's where they come from - - -

Now one place, they got two camps -
oil people, THESE people very good (Indicates by drawing in sand) -
they bring in two young fellas, you know -
to look out for their country -

When they finish -
when they finish -
he get 'nother two blokes come in -
what know THIS country again (Indicates further north)
Stephen: Yeah.
You see

Ah, all right -
when this two finish -

216

then he get 'nother two more man belongs to this country he must go
    that way bit more further, this two come back -
back to their home (Laugh) -
it's a thing like that -
these people -

But these other people (Indicates) workin' this way[99] -
they haven't got anybody
they just went on they own -
cutting line an' everything[100] -

So they musta knock some stone over -
'cos some stones, that snake you know (Laugh)[101] - - -
stone -
outside you can see it -

Sometime we want a rain we -
chip (Hits wood with tool) - -

Right! -
'We want rain in Broome' -
we say you know -
(Laughter)

Sometime we chip-im again (Hits again) -
we want rain here (Laughs) -
oh very big thing, you know (Laughs) -

Well somebody musta made a mess of this one -
you know these oil people didn't ask nobody -
they just went in they own ways -
never worry about, any Aborigines -
Looma people
Stephen: Yeah
Or find somebody - -

So when they alone that, that sun, cloud bin come right over -
right up -
an' I was sleeping here in dis, block out here you know, Coconut Well
country -

So - - - -
when I, when I seen this cloud it's only long like from here to, oh to the

217

wireless station, you know the old wireless station, that long -
but you know (Laugh) he's a cloud -
aah -

Ah -
when I get up night-time, I look, 'Hello, cloud, mm, very short one, that
    funny' -
so I come back to sleep -
I was thinking, 'Hello, something wrong -
might be my countryman somewhere' -

So I went, I get up again -
that thing was straight up -
but I see him he went down now next time I come out of the door -
going down in that reef -

'Aaaah must be countryman,' I say
Stephen: In the reef?
In the reef
Stephen: In the sea?
That reef, yeah -

'Aah must be my people -
somewhere,' I said you know? -
I told the little fellas, I with two little boys 'Here y'are -
see that one?'
'Yeah'
'That's my people' (Laugh) -
'Oh' -
'Snake' -
'*Yungurugu*' , I say, 'That's *yungurugu*' -
'Ah, oh yes,' two little boy watch everything, he going down - - - -

So three days after that, two or three days I think, three days -
this bloke picked me up - -
218
this fella picked me up, not THIS fella (Indicates), this fella -

'Cos he come to me all the time these people -
he must find out they might run over something -

So he took me, 'I'm going to Dampier Downs, to the camp, I gotta pick
    up them two boys, they finished now, you want to come with me?'

I said, 'Yes, I gotta go -
er might be something wrong with the country, my people (Laugh) -
my people,' I say, it's a spirit, you know?
Stephen: Yeah

And that was true -
we came up there -

So -
this two bloke give me a cup of tea and everything my people you know -
oh and some wild honey one billycan full (Laugh) -
big feed -
So they tell me, 'How these people, they good people?' -
'Oh very good, only THESE people no good -
you know what they done these people they went straight across the
    country -
never -
they got nobody with them -
they just help themselves anywhere' -
'Ooh' -

'You know what happen,' this other bloke tell me, 'You know what
    happen?' -
oooh he seen the cloud straight away coming -
straight across -
you know -

(Soft voice) I stop quiet, you know -
'What sorta cloud?' I said -
(Soft) oh you know (Laugh) -
'Yeah' - -
'Yeah' - -
'Ooh yeah' - -
'Ah' -

'An' where did he go?'
'I guess something wrong this side,' they said -
'Yeah -
yeah,' I said -
'I know,' I say, 'He come straight up -
to my place' (Laugh) -
you know they know my place too -

An' that's where he come down finish -
something wrong this end -
I dunno what gonta happen in the rain (Laugh)
Stephen: Yeah
Rain time -
might be - -
this cloud musta come just let me know -
something wrong
Stephen: Yeah

But once they start to bore -
that'll be the time (Laughter) -
you know
Stephen: For oil
For oil -

Today they only clearing -
but they musta knock something over -
stones, you know -

(Soft) So - -
that's the thing

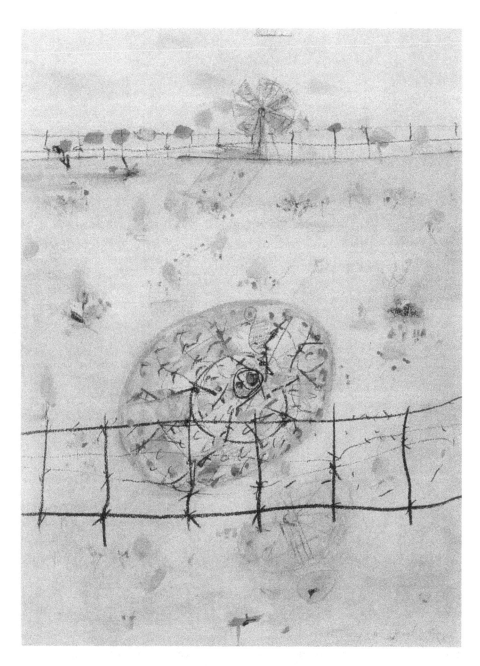

The Third Eye

1983, 76.5 cm x 57 cm, gouache and pastel on D 'Arches paper

Culture and the Modern Text

How is it possible to consider the present, and quite specific present, with a mode of thought elaborated for a past which is often remote and superseded?

Gramsci

Occasionally one comes across a fragment of writing or a photograph at the frontier of white and Aboriginal cultures which is striking in its modernity.[102] For instance, this moment in Grant Ngabidj's story from the East Kimberleys:

> *Topsy could ride a horse and had learnt very well to shoot blackfellers too. She was a school girl I think, brought up on*

a mission station like at Port Keats or Kalumburu. She used to carry two side revolvers and all bullets around her belt. Oh she was fucking dangerous I tell you.[103]

All of a sudden a new readibility is forged, but this is not a product of a mere chance encounter of harmonious individuals (Ngabidj and the reader): it depends on the ascendance of new ways of reading that can be easily identified. One is a rough-cut feminism (Topsy as the tough and unscrupulous man-killer) and another is the image repertoire deriving from Hollywood Westerns, Annie Oakley in particular.

Similarly, Paddy Roe's sunglasses install an extra dimension to his portrait. Butcher Joe looks astounded, and the next day will sport a flamboyant pair in imitation of this sign which had impressed me (in my 'modern' culture) and had caused me to make a flattering comment to Paddy Roe. So strategies already existed in the spoken dialogue which produced not only the photograph, but also a very transitory fad in sunglass-wearing down at *Mamabulandjin*. Later I was to find my sunglasses, which I had originally given to Paddy Roe to ease his eyestrain, all by themselves on a table at the Kool Spot restaurant. How did they get there?

My glasses have now become a clue in a detective story which only a Cliff Hardy or a Maigret from Broome could solve. The answer lies in a knowledge of that culture, and I will not give it here. My aim in writing is, after all, only to open enquiries—to ask questions, often of the wrong sort, in order *not* to be always condemned to ask the same questions. If one wishes to come to terms with Aboriginal modernity, it is necessary, first of all, to revise one's notions of Aboriginal culture, or even culture in general, and to see culture as *constructed* in contemporary *texts*. It also is necessary, as a part of this process, to work out one's political position in relation to culture. There is no other way in which to describe the ways in which people invest energy and money in *one* sort of culture while ignoring or even denigrating the other sorts.

The problem, therefore, with words like culture or society, is that they tend to be taken for granted as 'things out there' which are independent of the *positionality* of the person speaking and the *form* that the talk takes which represents that culture. Stuart Hall, a British intellectual who analyses media events, has pointed to the need to tell stories *in different ways* because one can't rely on language to carry one's intentions, or on the reader to faithfully pick up on that intention.

> *... the fact of course is that journalists of very different views and dispositions can tell the same kind of story. I often say to radical friends, 'I'm not interested in what a person's politics are; what kind of stories do they tell?' Because I know many*

radical journalists in the media who tell exactly the same sto-
ries: they construct events with the same kinds of languages
as the people who disagree with them profoundly. So there's
a kind of stabilisation in the institutions and in the available
discourses which are sustained in a set of known practices in-
side those institutions. Those stories, or rather those ways of
telling the stories, write the journalists. The stories are already
largely written for them before the journalists take fingers to
typewriters or pen to paper.[104]

What could be more predictable, then, than the following headline about an anthropologist:

ANU ACADEMIC CAUSES STIR ON FREE-SEX STUDY[105]

It causes one to ask what specific conditions make academic disciplines newsworthy. What communicative machine is tuned to detect in their quiet murmurings the words which can be amplified to reach wide audiences in newsprint or on the air? One answer emerges immediately: anthropology, as a science of Man, can finally speak the 'truth' about our sexuality by comparing it to that of the Others who are untransformed by the ravages the industrial West has wreaked on our humanity.[106]

One only has to connect the anthropological category of analysis called 'sexual behaviour' with sexuality as an object of financial and cultural investment (by business, the state, medicine, culture) to generate this amplification effect. Texts can then proliferate in a way not possible for other anthropological categories—a new way of analysing 'kinship' would hardly make the news today.

The article in question, on the front page of the *Advertiser* referred to Derek Freeman's book *Margaret Mead and Samoa: the Making and Unmaking of an Anthropological Myth.*[107] It contains a series of assertions as to what the Samoans are really like. According to Freeman, Mead 'really got it totally wrong' in her famous text of 1928, *Coming of Age in Samoa*. Mead's book, which was popularly read at that time as a manual for the 'permissive society', spoke of the Samoans condoning adolescent free love. Now Freeman, fifty years later, using different methods of analysis and drawing on a different range of data, comes up with a different set of results which he claims are in a closer relationship to the 'truth' of that particular society.

Neither of these anthropologists is 'right'. Societies are not fixed in atemporal states of objectivity waiting to reveal their truths through the anthropologist's impassive questioning. The 'society', whatever that is, shifts and changes according to the way in which the analytic gaze is directed. And then the anthropologists must speak, almost confess, in the halls of Western imperial power and tell the story of what they have seen. If what they say pleases, they will be rewarded. So what they say about the Others must be relevant to their own society. Margaret Mead's art and virtue was in her text; a utopic construction of a future Western society. Derek Freeman can reread her text if he wishes, but without basing his argument on a transcendent *reality* of Samoan society.

On the ABC's radio programme AM 108, an American colleague of Mead's was telephoned. His contribution was to attribute the difference of opinion between Mead and Freeman to individual *bias,* and these *individual* biases were 'opposite'.

Leaving aside the problem of the difficulty in occupying 'opposite' positions within the one discipline, one remains with the important dualism: individual versus society. The individual, that entity largely constructed in psychological discourses, now becomes the repository for 'error' (and therefore open to disciplinary correction); and truth is free to remain in society, to be eventually discovered by a less error-stricken anthropologist.

Individual 'bias' and social 'reality' are terms which can no longer be relied upon to stay in the one place. They are characters in a story which has been told too often to be of any further use. As Stuart Hall says, it is the way the story is told which is beginning to matter more and more. Paddy Roe's story, 'The Good Oil Company and the Bad Oil Company' is a story which is the product of his culture, it is a discourse which is at odds with the usual way in which mining exploration is talked about. For Roland Barthes, these different accounts circulate in a 'stray field', which is culture.

> ... *a unique object because there is nothing to oppose to it, an everlasting object because it never breaks; in short: a peaceable object inside which everyone can gather without apparent conflict. So where is the* work *that culture does on itself where are its contradictions? Where is its misfortune?*
>
> *In order to answer this, we must, in spite of the epistemological paradox of the object, hazard a definition—of the vaguest kind, naturally: culture is (what is known in magnetics as) a stray field. And of what? Of languages.*[109]

In Broome, the diversities and discontinuities of Australian culture are reproduced in the tourist shops where large revolving stands of postcards juxtapose images which create Broome as a specific locality at the same time as reactivating the tourist as subject, a subject which is supposed to slot into this environment in a particularly important way: tourism is Broome's major industry. This is perhaps the reason for the peculiar intensity with which tourists 'read' the images on these postcard stands.

'Seaside holiday' is represented by the British dirty-joke cartoon cards and by 'Surfers' bikini ones. The Aboriginal culture is coded exclusively in terms of a traditional and unified culture; the Aborigines shown might come from Central Australia or the Northern Territory, now both great centres for the reproduction of Aboriginal culture as a commodity. Romantic and anthropological discourses on Aborigines also aid this distancing and reconstruction of Aboriginal culture as past and thereby fixed. Cultural 'safety regulations' for postcard production make it impossible to produce postcards of, say, an Aborigine with Kelloggs for breakfast. The next card on the stand might be one of a Broome industry, the meatworks, pearling, or an offshore oil rig. All these industries are normalised for cultural consumption at the popular cultural level of the postcard. They all become equally part of the tourist-subject's world. Just as one accepts notions of Aboriginality as 'traditional', so too the appearance of American companies drilling for oil or gas on the North-West shelf passes under the sign of 'the normal', the unquestionable.

One way to read Paddy Roe's story about the oil companies is in terms of stark moral dualism: one company is nomadic—it stops and starts and accepts the custodianship of the two young Aboriginal men who change over for each stretch of country; the other is anti-nomadic—it just barges through. Representing searchers for oil in the Kimberleys according to this kind of structure in no way contests their presence as capitalist enterprises. Paddy Roe's narratives are not contestatory. As Barthes says, 'The question of *contestation* itself becomes a bourgeois idea'. But Barthes is talking about 'so-called developed countries' where, according to him, the proletariat has no culture of its own and its language is that of the lower middle class.

With Paddy Roe's story, it is easier for us to trace the history of his discourse in the traditional narratives of his area. The notion of two figures travelling together is present in the sacred story of the B ...... Here it is transposed to the two companies, then reverberates with the two young men travelling ahead and guiding the oil team, just like the two *maban* (clever men) who were the protective avant-garde when tribal groups used to travel on foot.

Moral dualism is also present in the traditional story of *Walibungu* and *Yarinyaribungu*, the good sister and the greedy sister. The two sisters are looking for bush onions *(yarinyari)*. The greedy sister finds a bed of nice big onions and starts digging them up with the digging stick. When she sees her sister approaching she sends her back to camp to pick up their firestick. While she is away the greedy sister constructs a snake out of bark and puts it across the track, and her sister is then too scared to cross over. Now they can be seen in the night sky as two stars separated for ever by a snake of stars. Cooking, an elementary cultural activity, is suspended in this story since *Walibungu* holds the fire, and *Yarinyaribungu* the uncooked food.

The moral injunction, as with so much of Aboriginal law, is to share and to share equally.[110] The bad oil company is also 'greedy', because it doesn't employ young Aboriginal men. Paddy Roe's practical concern for unemployment can thus be read into a story which has the structure of a traditional myth. This elaboration of the mythic structure is one way that an Aboriginal cultural hegemony can operate in the Kimberley discursive network.

What of white hegemony? It is certainly not a single force exerting a negative power from above, inevitably stamping out Aboriginal culture. Its languages and practices are very diverse and they endlessly construct difference. Projected on to a linear time scale, such as the calendar we are so familiar with, 'different' objects, 'different' languages and 'different' practices can be seen as succeeding each other according to an ideology of 'progress'. But culture, generally, wanes. It 'goes downhill'. That is why objects like oil rigs can't be called cultural in the dominant discourses on economic progress and regional development. A stone axe is cultural precisely because of its uselessness in the sphere of 'progress'.

Now that the term 'culture' has become too big because it includes everything, we are left without a limit which defines the use or usefulness of the word. We have to agree with Barthes that culture 'is … a highly paradoxical object: without contours, without any term of opposition, *without remainder*'. But seeing culture everywhere is at least an activity which is not predicated on practices of exclusion, practices which rank cultural products. Standing in a 'stray field' near Broome and seeing culture all around might seem like an act of smooth technology; a gaze which doesn't stop panning. But most technologies stop, break things up and select. Taking photographs of black people, they will tell you, requires a longer exposure; you have to slow the shutter or open the aperture. In the photograph of the children playing on the beach, the white child is underdeveloped, she barely makes it through the technical process. The image says that whites are just making an appearance on the Kimberley landscape. But it could also be read, humanistically, as a celebration of reconciled racial difference. Languages at war in a culture of peace?

INTERVIEW WITH PETER YU

(21.3.1983)

Stephen: In any discussion people speak from certain definable positions and I think we should make these positions clear at the outset. I'm someone who is interested in culture and communication generally and in the application of general ideas in these areas to the specifics of the Broome situation.

I'm interested in the way that cultural things interact with political things and I believe that people who deny the political importance of culture, who say that it's just for entertainment, would be masking the nitty-gritty of cultural definitions, promotions, funding procedures, even the role of certain individuals in securing a body of material or work which counts as cultural for a specific community.

So that's the position I want to talk from. I guess you'd be talking from the position of NAC representative for the region?[111]

Peter Yu: As that, but first of all as an Aboriginal person interested in cultural preservation or the rediscovering of cultural traditions.

So with your NAC position, does this mean that you have to be diplomatic in this interview?

No, nothing. I'm here as the representative of the communities that put me in the NAC, and I speak for them and no one else, not the government or anything like that.

I should get clear what area that is.

West Kimberleys, as far south as La Grange, east of Christmas Creek Station to Mt Barnett Station on the Gibb River Road.

And up Dampier Peninsular?

Yeah, it encompasses about twenty communities altogether, plus the three major towns of Broome, Derby and Fitzroy Crossing. It includes about six thousand people.

Yeah, that extends further east than the area that Paddy Roe defines as his traditional cultural area.

Oh, yeah. Most of my involvement with cultural things has been in the same area as Paddy. I went through the law with him.[112]

One of the questions I wanted to ask you was about 'multiculturalism'. You've got successive government policies which have been vaguely defined and sporadically implemented, like 'assimilation' in the early times, then 'integration'. Now the dominant ideological policy seems to be multiculturalism, the Grassby model. Is this a useful word to use in relation to the Broome situation?

It could be if people were fairly genuine, I mean I think most people would aspire to that sort of thing. I suppose multiculturalism means a lot of things: living in harmony or different mixtures of people, different races or different cultural backgrounds, I suppose a lot of people would aspire to that. But in reality it is a different thing. For instance in Broome I don't think that could be achieved. There are too many imbalances. Broome is always given as an example, people make it out to be a cosmopolitan, multicultural community. I personally think it's a lot of bullshit. And mainly because that particular word is being exploited, you know, financially. Some individuals.

How do they do that?

Well, through the tourist industry: the attractiveness of the perfect community, come and see how we live. It is a lot of bullshit because this community is controlled by one power group. And the power game they play is one of economics.

So you've got the same sort of capitalist forces operating here as elsewhere?

Yeah, well they're exploiting the principles of racial harmony or whatever you want to call it to further their own financial gains.

I suppose you can easily see the differences in living conditions which point to this class/race difference.

Exactly. I think racism is still fairly blatant. I see examples of it in this community two or three times a day. The only difference, and the reason why racism might not appear blatant to outsiders, is that there is a large coloured population in the middle that tends in some instances to act as a buffer zone between the whites and Aboriginal people. Because those coloured people have always been placed in a position where they've either been told to conform by the whites, to accept a sort of assimilationist policy, to aspire to the white values and to reject their other cultural background.

Can racism operate from their position towards other groups also?

231

Well it does. Initially it's forced upon them by the white people. For instance, you know when citizenship rights were brought in? Up to about 1968 before you were declared a citizen you had to apply to the government and you had to satisfy certain rules and one of those rules was that you weren't allowed to mix with full-blood Aboriginal people. This before you could be called a citizen and were entitled to receive a dog ticket which gave you drinking rights or whatever.

So this strategy effectively distanced some Aboriginal people from others who might even be members of their own families?

Yeah. Of course.

What about today? Does police surveillance as it operated then to change lifestyles and affect cultures still have the same effect?

Police? What do you mean police surveillance?

The reason I asked the question is that police activity in this town seems to be pretty intense; nightly visits to hotels, checking visitors coming in and out of town.

Well, that's not unusual for Aboriginal people. They always do that, every minute of the day. I suppose it's a similar thing for, um, some people call them hippies, I don't know the particular reason, but the heavy concentration is still on Aboriginal people. If you see a drunk white bloke in the street and a drunk Aboriginal bloke, you know which guy will get put into prison for that.

What about welfare work? Does that work tend to mould everybody to the same middleclass lifestyle? What sort of cultural consequences might this have?

Well, I think if you look at the whole history of the welfare movement, it works with a series of structured forces which have tended to break down traditional Aboriginal culture and lifestyle.

Could it be aligned in any way with the dominant racist ideas of society? Would welfare be on that side of the fence?

I would say generally yes, but I think that in the last five years in the Kimberleys there have been committed people, individuals within the welfare system who have been able to help in the development and

232

maintenance of culture. But the system as a whole has definitely had policies which have contributed to the breaking up of cultures.

You would agree then that is difficult to maintain the law, or keep a culture going in a racist context?

I think that would be difficult, to maintain it at the level that you would want to. But all the same I think there has been a resurgence as awareness increases among a lot of younger people.

In what form do you see culture expanding? Do you see it in the traditional sense of dance, song and ceremony, or in the sense of rock groups, football and so on?

I mean in both instances, I mean in the traditional sense through what we are participating in, and I also mean in the wider development sense where Aboriginal people are gaining a greater awareness and are wanting to be self-managed and independent and therefore wanting to have control over those cultural issues. Especially in the out-stations movement, you know, the communities moving back to their countries. That's one of the most powerful things happening in the resurgence of the culture. It brings back the structure, in part the disciplinary structure of the communities. Not only does it represent an independence from white rule, but it avoids the obvious sort of problems like alcohol and exploitation of women.
It restrengthens us.

Have a few been set up in the area you're looking after?

Oh yeah, well we had four communities squatting on pastoral reserves this year, without any assistance from the government, just living on the dole or pensions.

Were they interested in bringing back their culture to larger centres like towns?

Initially they had no alternative but to strengthen the culture within their own community. That's the first priority, afterwards they might be thinking of taking things to other places as a broader educational process.

What do you think about these festivals in town, the Shinju for instance? They seem to construct Aboriginal culture in a particular way, primarily as a spectacle to be consumed by a white audience.

Personally I don't agree with it. For instance, the Shinju committee in the foreword to their booklet don't recognise that Broome was built on Aboriginal land, or even that Aboriginal people are involved in the town itself, or even the area. It mentions all the others, the Asians, etc. It's not consistent, it's totally exploitative, like I was saying. It is not a matter of concern for the organisers or the people who come to see it. It's just a spectacle for that little moment, there is no insight into Aboriginal culture as a whole way of life.

Interview with Paddy Roe

Paddy: Yes, what else we was gonna talk about? Tell me what you want.

Stephen: Well, we've been right through that country now haven't we?

Yeah, we finish.

We might have to go back again and find something else we forgot about.

Yeah.

But that's good.

We been right through to the end of the country.

Thank you.

What about um, I might ask you a question.

Yeah.

You ever hear the word nomad?

Eh?

Nomad, you ever hear that word, nomad?

Mahomet?

No, nomad.

No maid.

No-mad.

No made.

Yeah.

Er no, oh I might have.

Well some people say that's the way Aboriginal people live.

Oh.

As nomads.

Oh no maids.

Nomads, they go, they don't live in house with garden.

Ooh yes yeah.

They move around.

Yeah move around all the time yeah that's right   that's right   Oh that's the er er that's what that word say?

Yeah.

Yeah yeah.

You think that's a good way to live?

GOOD way to live   that's the way we used to live   we go from place to place right around that place come back other side again (Laugh) 'til we come back to work   same thing.

But you still do it now, little bit.

Yes, we CAN do it   we do it too sometimes   when I take the childrens
out you know   few people go out   you know.

Oh yes   'nother las', oh two three weeks ago   they had two little boys and two old woman   the old woman is there now one of them   living

with me you know in ah   *Mamabulandjin.*
They went out you know   they stop, camp Saturday night one place
Sunday night 'nother place Monday they come back   'cos Monday was
holiday   an' they come back   er school Tuesday (Laughter).

You know   But that's the way the old people used to live   you know
we used to go   little mob here little mob there but we all one person
(Laughter)   you know?

Why we do this because if we all go in one mob you know not enough
to eat 'cos we gotta go in small mobs   to get enough feed   might be
two goannas, *barni* you know?   enough feed to this little mob that's
finish   next day we get 'nother two   so the food never go   short
always there   no good kill one place, lot you know   we gotta keep
some for next time   come 'round again (Laugh).

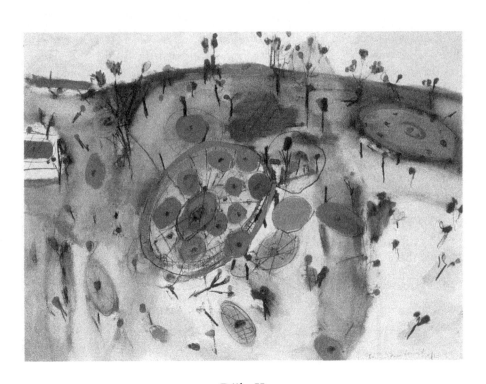

Djila II

1983, 57 cm x 76 cm, gouache and pastel on D'Arches paper

Strategic Nomadology: Introduction

But prison's nothing special
For any Nunga I know,
'Cos the white man makes his prisons
Most everywhere we go.
   Aboriginal Country and Western Song.

As we approach the end of this book, we find ourselves in a continuing movement of turning back towards places that are familiar to us, and thereby reflecting on our journey.[113] Not all the places were covered, even in Roebuck Plains, and Krim's painting/map (Page ii), made after a later trip to Broome, shows place names which only then came up in conversation between Krim and Butcher Joe. Real, no doubt, but also metaphorical, they trace the trajectory of their desire, as artists, to always go further, to clear a space for others to follow. All they are saying is 'Look, there might be something else'. This 'something' is like a point of expansion into which desire can flow and it is a strategic problem which asks *what can be done* in certain locations.

   Krim's painting/map (one signifier will not suffice), which opens the book, breaks the definitional rules, the rules of genre. It is not representational like a landscape, and it is not metrical (obeying grid squares) like a map. Its colours and lines flow around the contours of a country which emerges in the practices of conversation, including Butcher Joe's iconographic sand drawings. Later Paddy Roe contributed to it, so it follows Aboriginal understandings of representation (it is collectively produced) and is closer to Aboriginal iconography in its form than are Krim's other paintings.

   The painting/map draws together certain threads in this book, finding itself, in the end, with a quite different reading of the country; a subversion of the scientific map at the beginning of the book, and a 'total' representation now instead of the exploratory tracks of the different series of paintings. This is also the direction of the writings. Each

239

fragment looked for something, departing from a certain point, clearing a space in which to walk, then holding in abeyance and rarely uttering that artificial word 'nomadology' which would aspire to transcend all the fragments and dominate their significance.

It is an artifical word in the sense of 'artifice' or 'artifact'. It is the 'empty spindle' of Ada Janet Peggs; things can be formed around it, texts can be woven and put to use, but it means nothing in and by itself. It stands in for all those transcendent and general terms like Truth, Fact, the Dreamtime, Authority, Origins, Law and Order. And, of course, it is applied inappropriately to Aboriginal cultures, as the interview with Paddy Roe shows. It indicates the inappropriate application of any *singular* word to the lifestyle of a whole people. It is only within relations of power difference (colonialism) or knowledge difference (the social sciences) that a discourse can be mobilised as the *summary* account of a culture. But 'nomadology' is also an exotic import, from the writings of Deleuze and Guattari.[114] How did they see this 'empty spindle' being used? No doubt they would welcome its aberrant usage in the Kimberleys.

For them, nomadology is the study of nomadism (nomadism being more than just a way of life of a people) and it is a philosophy which has been developed in recent years by scholars looking for ways to contest the Graeco-Roman philosophical traditions which have grown up with advanced Western capitalism and continue to be its support. So it is more than a way of designating the 'behaviour' of a 'people', ie. as nomadic, as opposed to agricultural or sedentary-type peoples. These are the anthropological definitions of nomadism, ones that see nomadism as being a kind of second nature to a whole people. As long as whole races or communities can be designated or defined as being *of a certain sort,* then the grounds for racism remain intact. A counterstrategy is to call nomadism a *practice* and a *knowledge* potentially present in relation to any event, potentially effective in relation to *any* struggle for survival.

How does one find out about nomadism, or understand nomadology? Firstly, there are texts, written or unwritten, from other cultures which pre-date the philosophical texts of Western capitalism. In this sense the ways in which many Australian Aboriginal people speak are free of the categories which articulate Western philosophies. Secondly, there are ways of living which are organised around movement, change and local politics. Then there is the imagination of the writer whose art eschews author-ity. All of these contribute to the study of nomadism.

One of the concerns of nomadology is power and the way it works in the everyday lives of ordinary people. The workings of power depend to a certain extent on the social system in which one lives. It could be a monarchy, a feudal society or the modern industrial state. Power functions to fix people in relations of production; they must work *for* someone, and they must also defend someone else's territory. The evolution of the mechanisms of power has been shown as progressing towards greater and greater efficiency, towards increased *fixity* of the people *(what* you are, *where* you live, etc.) and towards greater surveillance of the people.

Imagine a pre-feudal or nomadic society in which people roam around in bands. How does 'someone in power' get these people to do things like work, go to war or even pay taxes? They are never in the same spot, and may even have ways of warning each other about the force which wants to subject them.

In monarchic societies the structure changes shape. There emerges a *hierarchy* of delegation of power, the king or queen at the top, and various lords who count as his or her representatives in the localities. Each person then becomes fixed in relation to a *centre* of power and knowledge. It is this centre which tells people what they are (knowledge) and what they must do (power) in order to gain a living. But this system was also inefficient, not only were there still bands of nomads, but the lines of communication from the 'top' to the 'bottom' were often hard to maintain. Police forces were introduced with networks of informers. Information control or surveillance thus became the tool of power throughout society as it moved into the twentieth century. In the modern state, positions such as monarch are no longer as important as the mechanisms, like surveillance, which hold people in relations of production. Schools, prisons and factories all discovered ways of exercising power through observation. One strategy was the arrangement of work benches in rows so that one person could maintain surveillance by walking up and down.

With these sorts of structures ruling people's daily lives, it is not so useful to imagine that power is 'held' by some position (like Prime Minister). The state maintains its economic operations through the proliferation of *strategies* like the above. Such strategies are supposed to increase efficiency and productivity for their own sake, though occasionally a moral discourse is also recruited, one which says that it is good for people to be hard-working, punctual, regular and neat. It is easy to internalise these beliefs, because they are so current, and it is also easy to imagine that nothing can be done because everything is controlled by 'those in power'. This is not the case. Power does not oppress from above, as it were; it is *exercised*. It comes into being each time a particular strategy is employed and contestation of these strategies can take place at a local level. This should not be misconstrued as a call for anarchy (like driving through red lights), but as a call for an intelligent appraisal of the everyday actions that people perform. Let those who 'hold office' continue their manoeuvres imagining that they wield a power which is as grand as their rituals of pomp and circumstance. Around them there is a cultural revolution generated by the perversity of popular movements, scattering off in all directions while state and business apparatuses slowly recuperate them and package them for the Culture industry.

Deleuze and Guattari wrote about those bands of nomads like Genghis Khan and his armies. They talk about them as 'war machines', and compare them to the sedentary organisation of the state. The war machine is always exterior to the sovereignty of the State. It is

> ... *a pure immeasurable multiplicity, a swarm, an irruption of the ephemeral at the same time as the power of metamorphosis ... It balances fury against measure, speed against gravity, the secret against the public, power against sovereignty, the machine against the apparatus ... the war machine is of another type, of another nature, of another origin compared to the state apparatus.*[115]

As the song quoted in our epigraph shows, Aboriginal people have been situated in a similar relation of *exteriority* to the workings of the state. But while the marauding armies of nomads like Genghis Khan have disappeared, and the conditions for their existence no longer pertain, nomadism as a set of practices still survives in all sorts of ways. Traditional ways of living have a habit of not dying off completely, even when modern society seems to have quite decisively closed the book on the past. They persist as ideas or as practices and even now the 'progress' we have made can be measured afresh in their light.

For the nomad, Australia is still not divided into eight 'states' or territories, it is crisscrossed with tracks. The smooth space of these invisible and secret tracks has been violently assaulted by the public chequerboard grid of the states. This means boundaries to be patrolled. One type of job for the first pastoralists was the boundary rider, the very symbol of our economy—lonely individuals obsessively marking out the boundaries of their territory, territory as land-capital, as culture-capital, as money-capital. Even now, those who resist living like middle class individualists are either seen as traitors, bludgers or as ignorant, for the knowledge of the nomad doesn't count as knowledge.

Just as it was said of Genghis Khan that he 'didn't understand' the phenomenon of the state, it has been said of the pearling Aborigines of the early days in Broome that they 'had little or no understanding of contracts binding them to the boats, or of monetary rewards'.[116] While looking ethnocentrically from the inside of one knowledge, the 'others' have only been defined in negative terms; it is now time to say what they *did* understand. The 'state' is a metaphor for the interiority, it stabilises a sense of presence, it knows 'exactly where it stands'. For the state, nomadism constitutes a threat from the outside (it is no accident that a Defence Department television advertisement shows us the coast-line of Australia: the opposite of the interior, Canberra *is* the interior). Nomadism, then, must be described in positive terms, not merely as the *lack* of Western advanced-capitalist characteristics. The citadels of the state distrust the nomads because they don't know where this other dynamism will lead. They can't reduce the activities of the nomads to just one effect, so that they can say, finally, *that* is what they are like, *that* is what they do all the time. The nomads guard their secrets, and they move too fast for the grounded organisation of the state.

Nomadic organisation is neither more primitive nor more evolved than State organisation. 'Primitive' societies have often been defined as societies without a State, that is, where distinct organs of power do not appear. But to conclude from this that in not attaining a degree of economic development they are below the level of understanding 'complex' state apparatuses is nonsense. Perhaps they are resisting that very formation. Even the notion of 'chief' or 'headman' is refused by Aboriginal societies in Australia. For instance, it was said in relation to Galarrwuy Yunupingu at a Central Land Council meeting that: 'The "Pitja" people in particular, felt "sorry" for Galarrwuy because of the burden he is forced to carry: speaking for everyone was "a heavy thing".'[117] In so-called primitive societies, nomadism may be one of the surest mechanisms which works against any formation of State apparatuses. It maintains the dispersal of groups and concentrates mechanisms of power within them and at a local level.

But nomadic organisations are not neatly opposed to state apparatuses, inhibiting their foundation. There have always been states or empires, and their exterior relations are either ecumenical relations (ones that link organisations on a world scale in-between States, like religions or multinational companies) or relations with neo-tribalism in the cities; gangs, gang warfare, social 'cliques' and so on. Nor is the interior/exterior division a permanent one. Nomadism has always infiltrated even the heart of government. There is, for instance, the swarming and ambiguous group of the *lobby*—sometimes comprised of members holding state positions, sometimes not, trading in favours and secrets, always mobilised towards specific tasks. The two groups, government and lobby, are dependent on each other for their mutual functioning, yet they are animated by different sorts of *esprit de corps,* they have many characteristics which are opposite. The lobby has 'secret' workings, while government presents public positions. This points to a quite different handling, or even definition, of information. In one sense, government no longer deals in information which is dynamic and effective; it functions to display information in order to 'hold' a situation. It advertises a strict hierarchy of power positions, whereas the lobby group works with a secret solidarity, a fraternity in which each person is on the same level, and which can go underground at any time.

Kinship is of relevance here. The dominant metaphor or model for kinship is the vertical hierarchical model of the *tree*. With patriarchal society, power relations, as well as family names, descend hierarchically from the forefathers. This model has been taken over in the structural organisation of the state and of bureaucracy. But a more frequent and nomadological function of kin relations is to establish *sideways* relations, links between different family groups on the basis of belonging to clan or 'skin' groups. (Deleuze and Guattari have found another plant metaphor for these sorts of relations: the *rhizome*, the bulb-like growth which can link any point with any other point, rather than connections proceeding by division from higher points to lower points.) Through skin-group categories, virtually all blacks in Australia can establish significant and specific relations with one another, eg. 'wife' or 'brother' among people who meet even for the first time. This, if nothing else, can be a basis for solidarity, contrasting with the practice of white historians, who, when constructing 'family trees' for Aboriginal groups stress linear time depth bringing with it an ideology of origins. The use of sideways or non-hierarchical kin relations is a traditional strategy for getting around official rigidity. Getting a sister who is in an official position to do something special for you is, by definition, anti-state.

Deleuze and Guattari talk about a separate kind of nomadic science which is creative, it keeps inventing things by *bricolage;* but each time the science of the state imposes its order of measured reason and appropriates them. This process is most visible at frontiers where knowledges which previously had only a local distribution are gathered up and generalised by the State. Vagabond knowledges are thus made respectable, visible and fixed in place.

Then there is the problem of work. In Broome the prison population is mostly composed of young Aboriginal men. These men are employed on various public works around the town, and this cheap labour is a continuation of the exploitation of blacks in Broome since the time of the earliest white settlement: 'blackbirding' for the pearl fleets, unpaid work on stations, minimally paid work in towns. When blacks around Broome could make enough money *not* to have to work for Europeans for rations this was largely based on prostitution for the pearling crews. Their economic independence caused the women to be driven out of town, according to a report of 1903, because the townspeople couldn't 'get hold of a native willing to work'.[118]

Work is a modern invention and it involved the capture by the State of an 'amateur' activity (a necessary or pleasurable activity) and its professionalisation. According to Geoffrey Blainey, there is ample evidence that Aboriginal nomads led a more leisured life than their European counterparts of, say, 1800.[119] With the imposition of the State apparatuses on the nomad patterns of life, leisure starts to be redefined as employment to the extent that the hegemony of the State is in operation. Any reassertion of nomadism can disrupt this hegemony, both work and unemployment disappear at the same time, and the nomad can continue to *follow* the local tracks, following the flux of matter that keeps one alive. For example, prospecting is, in this way, not unlike traditional food gathering. The value that the West places on precious minerals allows for a diversion and a resuscitation of nomadism in prospecting.

Nomadism used to have control of certain knowledges. We know about the problem that the states have always had with guilds; groups of nomads or itinerants who kept secret and among themselves their knowledge of masonry, carpentry or glassmaking. One of the principle tasks of the state has been to fix the workforce, to make it more immobile, to regulate the movement of workers and to exploit labour recruited in particular places like plantations, sheltered workshops or prisons.

So instead of organised banks of skilled workers travelling the countryside and taking up a contract for work which they could manage themselves (like the *compagnons* in Europe who made Gothic cathedrals), the State intervened to disqualify or make unskilled the great body of workers so that the wedge of a division of labour can be driven between them: intellectual/artisan, governor/governed. In this sense the workers now need the state in order to know what to do. The science of the nomadic skilled worker is vague (vagabond) and inexact. It is like the functionally exact impressionistic map opposed to the metrically exact map.

The sovereign science (of the city) and the nomad science (of the desert) are also opposed in the sense of vertical versus horizontal. The space of the city is crisscrossed with verticals which depend on gravity and on metaphors of hierarchy—one above the other. It is a space of pillars. It is crossed by falling bodies, the distribution of things in parallel lines. Gravity conditions metric and arborescent multiplicities (gravity is also a condition of the tree, and the tree is a metaphor for sovereign science—Darwin's evolutionary tree, Chomsky's grammar, genealogical trees, classificatory diagrams, orders of command in hierarchical organisations).

Poor 'Sorrento', a nomadic machine finally come to ground. It is named after a pleasure spot on the Italian Riviera. The name thus traces a link between nineteenth and twentieth century styles of tourism.

The smooth space of the nomad (Roebuck Plains) is a space of infinitesimal contact between bodies, rather than a visual space which can be broken up into grid squares. Its multiplicities are rhizomatic (going in all directions, any point connecting with any other point, as opposed to the branching structure of the tree).[120] These multiplicities occupy the space without counting it and one can only explore it in the act of travelling across it. It is rapid rather than grave. The State has 'gravity'. The slow work of putting up fences, making roads, crisscrossing the smooth space can be destroyed in seconds with the celerity of the turbulence of the cyclone, willy-willy, or flood.

To this can be related two ways of producing culture. Either one can 'reproduce' or one can 'follow'. The theoretical space which takes as its conditions of operation the constants of gravity and metrics reproduces the same objects continually, mechanically, professionally:

> *Reproduction implies the permanence of a fixed point of view exterior to the reproduction: looking at the flow, while being on the bank. But following is something different from the ideal of reproduction. One is certainly forced to follow when one is in search of 'singularities', matter and material rather*

than the discovery of a form, when one escapes the force of
gravity to enter a field of rapidity; when one stops contemplat-
ing the running away of a flux in a determined direction, and
one is carried away by a turbulent flux; when one is engaged
in the continual variation of variables rather than trying to
extract a constant, etc.[121]

In Aboriginal practice following is 'tracking up', hunting, discovering a singularity. In the Aboriginal science of tracking, following someone's footsteps means to 'know' the person. To walk exactly in their footsteps means that there is an imitation—not a reproduction—of the whole movement of their bodies. And for this reason Aboriginal groups know how to walk together, their bodies have the same movement, a technique which will assure that they stay together over long distances. The walking eccentricities of city people are adapted for short displacements, individual journeys (they can't walk together because of their different styles), they are mostly sitting.

The idea of *reproducing* culture, to produce things exactly according to a predetermined plan, an engineer's model, comes dangerously close to the idea of purity of reproduction in a racial sense. For this reason one must be careful to keep separate nomadism and race. There are no races of nomads, only peoples who practise nomadism. These nomadists can be found in any place (gangs and cliques in cities, as was pointed out above). To raise the question of race is to raise the question of racism, and one of the features of racism in dominant cultures is that it can only recognise 'race' among the minority or oppressed groups:

... the question of race only arises for inferiors or minorities.
A race is not defined by its purity, but on the contrary by the
impurity which a system of domination confers on it. Bastard
and half-caste are the true names of race.[122]

So in racist discourse, a white 'bastard'—some Scottish, French and Australian mix—can try to disqualify an Aborigine from 'serious' cultural qualifications, from Aboriginality, because of his or her 'mixed' genealogy. Only the dominant class can call the others 'half-castes'. Nomadism is not endemic to race; it is embodied in the way of life of a people and this way of life is a culturally acquired thing. It is the existence which is most suited to the country, to smooth spaces like deserts, steppes and the sea.

Even if the waterholes, the availability of water, determine where one must go, the points are still subordinate in importance to the voyage itself: this is a principle of nomadism. The trace is more significant than the point. The waterhole is both destination and place-to-be-left. Even when one is there one is about to leave: the life of a nomad is *intermezzo*.

247

The nomad does not try to appropriate the territory, there is no sense of enclosing it and measuring it as did the early surveyors. What is important to know are the ways of representing the tracks which cross it. The nomad does not have the sedentary function of

> giving people a measure of enclosed space, assigning to each person his or her section, and in regulating the communication between them. The nomadic trajectory does the contrary; it distributes people (or animals) in an indefinite, non-communicating open space.[123]

There is thus a great difference between city spaces and the plateaux, hinterlands or deserts which surround them:

> The sedentary space is crisscrossed, by walls, enclosures and paths between enclosures, whilst the nomadic space is smooth, marked only by 'traces' which wear away and move about with different trips.[124]

In spite of this, it is not correct to identify the nomad solely with movement. The nomad is, in fact, the one who *doesn't* leave the country. The migrant might leave a country embittered, never to return, and then try to appropriate the nomadic spaces of another country. In this the nomad is different from the migrant. S/he is always coming and going, but more or less in the same place:

> The nomads live in these places, remain in these places, and make them grow themselves in the sense that one notices that they make the desert no less than they are made by it.[125]

Paddy Roe's story about the hill that moved, shows how the land can change within a lifetime, and how that land, its signficance and the form it takes in discourse, are a product of his community and family. The existence of the red hill and the billabongs is a function of his father's dreaming. It is examples like this, infinite and successive *local* operations which link a specific place with a story or song (in other words, with processes of meaning) which work towards an absolute, but not universal, nomadic way of life. These successive local operations, which may also include solving of problems along the way, militate against any generalised operations like the State, like monotheism and other large apparatuses. One of the fundamental tasks of the State is to:

> ... crisscross the space over which it reigns, or to use smooth spaces as means of communication in the service of crisscrossed spaces, not only to vanquish nomadism, but to control migrations ... for this it needs fixed trajectories, with well-determined directions which limit speed, regulate traffic,

248

relativise movement and make detailed measurement of the
relative movements of subjects and objects.[126]

All this is 'police' work, in the broadest sense. The word police comes, of course, from the Greek for 'city', *polis*. Outside of the *polis* is the *nomos*, the land of the nomads, the smooth space. The nomadic rock group from Broome, *Madja*, sings a song about police *(lindju)* which complains of police harassment; their song writers recognise the specific mechanisms of control of flow, of segmentation, of limitation of speed imposed by 'police' work of any sort, from the Catch 22 of not being able to get a job without working experience to the idea of traffic lights in the big city (there are no traffic lights within two thousand kilometres of Broome):
When you start to move,

You can't get very far;
You're lost in a jungle of cars,
While the traffic lights tell you what to do:

See a green light,
yellow light,
red light,
stop …

Don't walk.

Nomads become creators of an absolute sense of speed, nomadism becomes synonymous with speed, the engulfment of smooth spaces, while the State as engineer precisely controls these spaces:

> *And every time there is an operation against the State, a lack*
> *of discipline, an uprising, a revolutionary or guerilla act, one*
> *could say that … a new nomadic potential is reappearing with*
> *the reconstitution of a smooth space or of a way of being in*
> *the space as if it were smooth.*[127]

The crowd, Elias Canetti pointed out,[128] had a power beyond that of its individual members and a logic of movement (sticking together and 'swarming') which can *get things done in* ways which overthrow 'proper channels' and 'standard procedures'. The collective will of a crowd *demonstrates* its symbolic right to occupy a space in which to live, to overthrow a corrupt government, to escape from poverty: nomadology studies the possibility of this collective will, a will which can only be sustained under conditions of necessity and whose potential for destruction in the modern age is no doubt a product of people being unused to living as a crowd. Even if they live in crowded conditions they are always being counted and told they are 'free' *individuals*.

The interrogation of black man by white man in Australia has always been, and continues to be, an interrogation about quantities: 'How far? How many? How long?' The vague (vagabond) responses of the noncounting nomads are frustrating for the white who has to quantify in order to reproduce. The multiple events of the nomad's world are illustrated in terms of specific, contingent and colliding singularities. (*When was that cattle station set up? Same time as that comet fell down [Halley's comet].*) In Aboriginal country beings 'swarm', they circulate in 'mobs' (most often 'big mobs'). In Aboriginal warfare *(daman)*, one group swarms and engulfs another group. It employs different tactics and technologies to those warfares which have had metallurgy at their disposal. Deleuze and Guattari have had to explain the triumph of the nomadic armies which crossed Europe and Asia in terms of a significant metallurgical skill: armaments had to be forged *en route*. Accordingly, they pay much more attention to the marauding, invading, destroying aspect of nomadism than to its alignment with the natural movements of seasons and the search for food. There is a good summary treatment of this latter aspect of nomadism ('The Logic of Unending Travel') in Blainey's book on Australian prehistory.[129]

As Blainey was careful to point out, the traditional black Australian was a technician of fire.[130] Always travelling with fire, these groups would make it suddenly spread and occupy the smooth spaces, flushing out game. The smoke from the fires were also a means of communicating, indicate direction of travel by one group, or the same group could communicate about the movement of a third group.

In addition to this, the nomadic Australian utilises two inventions, two creations of nomadic science to combat the speed of animals. The two projectile weapons (spear with spear thrower, boomerang) give man the advantage over the speed of the animal with the mechanical advantage of the spear thrower (it doubles the action of the arm in throwing) and the aeronautic advantage of the boomerang (the air can support it and bring it back). The pleasure of making the artifact is doubled by its successful projection and tripled when the game is eaten. The arithmetic is hardly that of the sport industry with its competitive base (*one* winner, disappointed second and third placegetters).

The weapon then merges with the tool in the sense that the same object may be used for different tasks, like the spear thrower as the moveable element of firesticks or the boomerang as a small shovel. But the use of objects as tools did not necessarily create work.

More generally, tools and weapons are the artifacts produced by the articulations of desire. Following the flux of matter, the nomad finds the desire for food *linked with* the animal via the spear cum spear thrower as precisely as there are linkages between other sorts of machines. Desire has nothing to do with a natural or spontaneous determination, the only desire is the one which is articulated, ie. spoken, joined, represented. Now these desires can be articulated together, organised, stratified, converging in relation to the flux of matter, such that a group tends to produce the same sorts of artifacts, artifacts which belong to the country.

> *Articulations can be grouped in huge ensembles which constitute 'cultures' or even 'ages'; they don't differentiate the phylum or the flux, dividing it into so many diverse phyla, of a certain order, at a certain level, and introducing selective discontinuities in the ideal continuity of the moving matter.*[131]

Here 'phylum' refers to a lineage or evolution of a certain line, like the one which must trace the link between the kettle and the internal combustion engine. Following the availability of materials and the form of the country, constantly repeated techniques articulated with the machinations of desire produce a slowly transforming series of artifacts, ones which are paradoxically mobilised with great speed in each instance and abandoned after they have served their (contingent) function. The book has appropriated nomadology as a metaphor, as an idea and a way of being. A fluid, turbulent model or framework for understandings, it opposes itself to the gravity and rigidity of the State and its 'professional' functions of segmentation, generalisation and fixing. It seeks to comprehend 'amateur' cultural production and distribution as *phyla in flux* articulated by desire. Photographs, paintings and spoken or written texts are artifacts appearing in phyla such that the words one utters are articulated with a desire that moves them along a line already traced by someone else's quite similar words. Similarly, a phylum of landscape painting links the colours and forms of a tradition of painting almost as concretely as if there were a vein of mineral colours being mined for ideas by Landscape Painting, a desiring machine moving across the country tracing a creative line of flight, a smooth space to move around in.

It is the country, therefore, which slowly produced the nomadism of the Aboriginal peoples who had lived there for so long. It was not they who suddenly decided to choose among a variety of 'social systems' and found nomadism to be the most suitable. The elements which go to make up a lifestyle are more practical and specific than that; they are strategies of survival, but at the same time produce pleasure in life.

If our book has succeeded in making some of these strategies visible we believe that it is because our approach has refused to be singular, it is because we know we are not 'right', it is because we have seen words and images only in relation to other words and images, moving on down the line. And then there was Desire, pushing us from the start, telling us we had to keep going, keep going until we got there. But where exactly is that?

251

Faced with the end of a book and the desire to continue, we can only transform ourselves and then disappear along well-established lines, remaining

[signatures]

S. Muecke

Paddy Roe

POSTSCRIPT: WRITING THIS BOOK

Interview with Stephen Muecke
(Fremantle Arts Centre Press, October 1984; interviewer B R Coffey)

Now that we can look back over this representative journey and over the 'country' that has been explored and opened up, as a kind of editorial postscript can we perhaps consider some important questions that relate to the process of writing this book?

Yes, of course.

Would you agree that the 'journey as book', the manner in which the literal and imaginative journeys across the country of the various contributors have been represented, has essentially been your responsibility? Most of the other contributions were created and exist primarily outside the book and it is your work of selecting, editing, interrogating and theorising which has created the narrative framework for the stories, songs, paintings, the geological and historical accounts to be given expression in this form.

Yes, I feel I do carry this major responsibility, and I am assuming it is not without problems. I am hesitant about taking on the label of 'author', and not just because of the trendy 'death of the author' slogan. I have been trying throughout to defer my authority by showing where my words came from, and where more of the same might be found. This disperses my authority throughout a community, a community of post-structuralist scholars and critics who form a movement in this country. I'm glad that I can take this opportunity to show how I think *this* author is inserted into the reading and publishing practices specific to the cross-cultural encounter in Australia. I think these questions are more important than my centrality or the others' relatively more marginal positions in relation to the production of the book.

253

It would seem that another very important 'truth' in this text is the approach you employ 'to construct a unity or general direction for the book'?

Yes, it is also true that there is an approach which I adapted from Deleuze and Guattari. I have shown where it comes from and have endeavoured to be open about the kind of philosophy it reproduces. And in the way that the book is presented it is intended that the reader be aware of this and feel encouraged to consider, question and even debate such matters.

But the main experiment I wanted to perform was one which asked if it would be possible for the country to 'write itself', and I think it worked. In the end there is an *archive* of fragments which are representative of just about everything that has been said about Roebuck Plains. There is a unity in that each fragment is contingent upon the place, at one time or another. As you say, the general direction is also an even more familiar narrative one, the story about three guys setting off on a journey ... but I hope it's clear that we take an ironic distance on this sort of narrative. More importantly, I think there is a theoretical impulse to this journey. The notion of abandoning our 'intellectual baggage' at the beginning (Krim and I had a big argument in which he used 'intellectual' as a swearword, just to force me to leave behind my certainties about what the book was already going to be) cleared the way to pick up another story, a story which incorporates the idea of not quite doing what one set out to do ... with 'nomadology', the relationship between the subject who is looking and the object being regarded is constantly shifting, and this effect is incorporated into nomadological theory, that is, a theory which recognises its limits, knowing that its object, always smarter than any subject, remains partially impenetrable.

You say at the beginning of the book that you, Krim and Paddy are all 'foreigners', 'remaining forever partially ignorant of the purposes and effects of the other's work'. But in the sense in which the book is its own country and that the philosophy and theoretical writing that you use mark its boundaries, Krim and, to a much greater extent, Paddy have to place much more trust in you than you do in them.

As 'foreigners', we run the constant danger of getting into trouble with the authorities in each others' countries. Who is there, at the cultural 'borders', to make sure our papers are in order? Yes, we have had to take each other on trust, knowing that there will be those who say we have betrayed each other, or even stolen across enemy lines. Most of the burden of this responsibility rests with me, since the book was largely out of Paddy Roe's hands as soon as he had finished putting his stories down on tape, except for the sustained influence he has had over me for the past ten years. And the writing was not Krim's responsibility, except to the extent that some of it was sparked by discussions about the book, specifically, and, once again, by the way we have been talking for nearly ten years. Krim also, of course, read and responded to the manuscript in various of the draft stages and approved the final draft. But, this responsibility for the writer is made more acute because of the political emphasis of the book, and I have tried to delineate our differences rather than stress our common purpose, for there is no absolutely common purpose, just as there is no common feature, like our humanity, which could adequately unite us for any common purpose.

This leads to one of the difficulties for the book. There is no equivalent to you interrogating Paddy or Krim, or commenting on their work; to Paddy responding to 'nomad'. Obviously in agreeing to do this interview you recognise this problem and the need to address it. But can this difficulty in authorial relationship finally be resolved?

Yes, your question raises a big problem, to which I think I can respond. We three are doing work which belongs to radically different social spheres. Paddy Roe lives in Broome where there is very little of the academic debate with which I am familiar. He asked me to write a book about his country, the three of us discussed the shape of the book, the notion of reading, and so on. I explained that I thought some of Paddy Roe's readers, Aboriginal people, would be happy to read what he had put down, 'but wouldn't know what the white fella was on about'. But I'm sure Aboriginal opinion on Krim's and my own contribution will be formulated, and those Broome people will get back to us on that. But it should be clear that I am in no way a spokesperson for that Aboriginal opinion, or its interpreter. I would never want to take on the undignified attitude of speaking on their behalf. For Paddy Roe one of my functions is that of the scribe, just as I was also his 'driver'—a specific job up in Broome. He was in charge of the words, I operated the machinery (taperecorder, car, typewriter) to move them around.

Having stressed the differences among us, I should also try to explain how I conceived of it as a cooperative effort, how it could be at all possible for us to work together. In one way the production of books from encounters at cultural frontiers is in an anthropological tradition. I am part of that tradition in the sense that it provided the structure which got me up to the Kimberleys in the first place. Now I have turned it around in a critical movement, which is also typical of many Aboriginal peoples' responses to anthropology, to the extent that I can go through the motions of working for Paddy Roe while I am working for an institution which is liberal enough to let me do that. Social scientific discourse is critised because of its virtual and exclusive presence on Aboriginal land and the way it used to pronounce so confidently the 'truths' of Aboriginal culture.

In another sense, if I were to write, and place my words next to Paddy Roe's, how was I to choose among the alternative texts which I could write? I couldn't just frame his words, explain them and otherwise disarm them by normalising them socially. I wanted to write in such a way that they would remain prominent in all the force of their opinion. His is a discourse of *affirmation*—you will have noticed how little he negates things. And this may be set against the successive negations of my post-structuralist theory, which functions, I hope, to clear away the debris of ways of talking which impose on, interpret, remove or just ignore the words of Aboriginal peoples. My problem was how to *rewrite* the Aboriginal-white encounter, while Paddy Roe has always been *talking* about just that, telling stories in joyous affirmation of his peoples' will to survive.

These stories will become more and more important as people realise the strength of the authority with which they are uttered. Paddy Roe trusted Krim and myself to provide a context for his words, and we have done, to the best of our abilities, what we knew how to do, working in our own spheres of activity.

However, despite this I still think that my work encloses Paddy's and Krim's too much. I *have* pronounced on Krim's but said very little about Paddy's: other critics will pick up on them more than me—Paddy and Krim are going to offer up much more beneath the surface which I only uncovered slightly.

Central to the book is your notion that within the concept of nomadology is to be found an appropriate way of responding to the places we live in, to the place we call Australia. What makes a series of things like the marginal, the fluid, the fragmentary an aesthetically preferable set of forms? A preferable way of thinking, of seeing and knowing?

I have not, of course, made any claims for Australians having an essentially nomadic way of life. The word is used metaphorically. And it is an expression of the last wave of criticism, literary and cultural, to emerge here (under foreign influences as usual). I am speaking of post-structuralism and post-modernism. The book is an instance of that sort of criticism, but grounded in practice, a concrete carrying-through of those ideas.

This new critical culture (some would say new orthodoxy) is having its moment of theory now, trying to shift the terms of the debate—for instance, as I have attempted to do, away from 'Man' and towards 'the Country', away from 'Society' towards 'Discourse'. And since these shifts have not yet gone to completion as *we* are as yet carrying out a struggle within the academy, then the marginal, the fluid, the collective are the more appropriate terms to use. And to the extent that they contain an energy, a vitality, perhaps a joy, they are aesthetically preferable.

Generally, certainly in the first two-thirds of the book, your approach is to be fairly open, empirical and questioning, only occasionally bringing the reader 'to a halt by a fence' with a very specific response, theory or attitude. But then, by the time we arrive at your final two essays you have gradually become quite specific in suggesting an appropriate theoretical basis for answers, and even appropriate responses, to the questions explored by the book. Why is this?

I wanted the book to be a kind of dialogue with the reader, and resisted to the end the notion of closure. But when you do pose questions, people will be unsatisfied if you fail to provide any sort of positive response. I wanted a reader who would become the prey of the text, seduced by its movement, reaching a breathless and mobile conclusion, ready for action and debate in relation to those issues which are most pressing for our survival in this country. The later fragments may seem too theoretical to some but in my opinion theory is not all that abstract, theories are the readily available frames in which certain questions and assumptions are allowed, and certain statements can appear ... in this way they have concrete effects.

Krim has told me he is very happy with the final draft of the book. He is pleased that it engages the reader in dialogue, that it gives proper emphasis to poetic and aesthetic understandings, that it is a positive and quiet book —things he feels are appropriate to the country and to nomadic understandings. But what about Paddy? Krim has said that he, and presumably you too, discussed the problem of 'foreignness' to each others' purposes and effects with Paddy at some length. How did he respond?

I'm afraid I honestly can't remember that specific discussion.

I'm not certain that the reference is to any one discussion. But according to Krim, Paddy said that his interest in doing the book was to keep his culture, the Aboriginal culture, alive and that as long as what you did supported that intention, it was all right.

Yes. We were very concerned that the book be supportive of that intention and I believe that it is. Of course you have no final control over the way others will want to perceive your work or the directions in which they will want to take it. In the end, what you hope for is that the book will at least encourage public debate, and also support from other directions, support which, as I have suggested, can lead to some kind of meaningful and useful basis for our understanding of the country.

NOTES

1. 'Yawur' has been variously spelt as 'yaour' and 'yawuru'.
2. By 'ideology' I do not mean 'dogma'—a way of labelling the talk one disagrees with—nor do I mean 'that which is false'. I mean something equivalent to 'commonsense'; the ideas a group takes most for granted, like the importance of being, and acting like 'an individual'.
3. See Gilles Deleuze and Felix Guattari, 'Traite de Nomadologie: La Machine de Guerre' in *Mille Plateaux* (Paris: Editions de Minuit, 1980) pp.434-522.
4. Paddy Roe, *Gularabulu,* (Fremantle: Fremantle Arts Centre Press, 1982).
5. William Dampier, *A Voyage to New Holland, The English Voyage of Discovery to the South Seas in 1699* (Introduced and edited by James Spencer) (Gloucester: Alan Sutton, 1981), p.120.
6. Thanks to Kevin Harris for this geographical expertise.
7. Dampier, *op. cit.,* pp.121-4.
8. Robert M Dixon, *The Dyirbal Language of North Queensland.* (Cambridge: Cambridge University Press, 1972), p.29.
9. Butcher Joe says that certain spirits (Ngadjayi) live near the shells at *Mimiyagaman*. Significant to his claim, is that these spirits are normally seen jumping off the crests of waves, especially if one sits all alone and very quietly at a place like Riddell Beach. According to Butcher Joe, these spirits become friendly with regular attention.
10. P E Playford, et al., 1975: 'Phanerozoic', in Geology of Western Australia. *Geol. Surv. West. Aust. Mem.* 2, pp.223-435.
11. J J Veevers and A T Wells, 1961: 'The geology of the Canning Basin, Western Australia'. *Bur. Miner. Resour. Aust. Bull.* 60, p.323.
12. Playford, et al., *op. cit.*
13. V Semeniuk, 1980: 'Quaternary statigraphy of the tidal flats, King Sound, Western Australia'. *J. Roy. Soc. West. Aust.,* 63, pp.65-78.
14. Semeniuk, *op. cit.*

15. Playford, et. al., *op. cit.*
16. Semeniuk, *op. cit.*
17. Playford, et al., *op. cit.*
18. Semeniuk, *op. cit.*
19. J N Jennings and R J Coventry, 1973. 'Structure and texture of a gravelly barrier island in the Fitzroy estuary, Western Australia, and the age of mangroves in the shore dynamics'. *Mar. Geol.*, 15, pp.145-167.
20. In recent years, cattle have trampled the borders of the waterhole. In the old days, a clear pool of water used to be visible.
21. The botanical reading of the Roebuck Plains has it that the Plains are 'saline short-grass plains, which occupy half the total area (of the coastal plains) on flats lying slightly higher than the zone of periodic inundation. The dominant species is *Sporobolus virginicus* forming a dense grassland fifteen to thirty centimetres tall. Associated plants are largely absent except for occasional clumps of samphire, also Bassi spp., *Eragrostis flacata*, and in shallow drainage lines *Dichanthium fecundum* and *Salsola Kali*. A change of slope, often abrupt, forms the inland boundary of these grasslands and is commonly marked by a dense but narrow band of *Melaleuca* low forest or thicket which may attain four to ten metres in height. 'Speck and Lazarides give the dominant species as M. *acacioides*. Shrubs such as *Acacia* or *Pandanus* spp. are rare to absent. There is a grass layer which may contain *Chrysopogon* spp. *Dichanthium fecundum* and *Sehima nervosum* or *Serochloa barbata*. X. *Imberbe, Aristida hygrometrica* and *Sporobuius virgincus*.' From J S Beard, *Vegetation survey of Western Australia* (Perth: University of Western Australia Press, 1979), p.84.
22. When Paddy Roe and Butcher Joe were boys, they used to mould little animals with the thick black mud at *Djarrmanggunan*.
23. Butcher Joe was the oldest boy. When he stopped doing it, the younger ones ('behind mob') took over.
24. Paddy Roe has spotted goanna *(barni)* tracks. This is the animal he most often hunts. He has to avoid the meat of 'woolly' animals like the kangaroo because he is in mourning. He has been for many years.
25. In the first decades of this century, when the first generation of part-Aboriginal children was appearing, the practice of the authorities was to collect the children and send them to Beagle Bay mission, north of Broome. This practice effectively blocked their traditional education. This book would never have been possible if Paddy Roe had not avoided the police.
26. They were heading south-east towards Thangoo Station.

27. Aboriginal English does not indicate gender in the pronoun. 'He', therefore, is 'mother'.
28. The sense of 'outa' would be 'out from under him'.
29. One of Paddy Roe's first experiences, like the experiences recounted in his dreaming stories, is made to seem like a *transformation*.
30. This story is a 'true story' (as opposed to a mythological or 'dreamtime' story—usually referred to as *bugarrigarra*). It is 'history' in the sense that it describes the early days of settlement of the sheep station from an Aboriginal point of view.
31. Mount Anderson station is in traditional *Nyigina* country. (See map on p.53.)
32. I had mistaken this story for the *Duegara'* story appearing in Paddy Roe's first book, *Gularabulu (op. cit.)* pp.19-28.
33. The word 'in' here means 'in the same place' as the house, or even 'under' the house.
34. *Gardiya* means 'white fellas'. My confusion is due to ignorance. If I had been listening to the story from the point of view of Paddy Roe's culture, I would have understood that 'these fellas' referred to the only other important characters apart from the people; the rainbow snakes.
35. That is, the snake which the *maban* from Mount Anderson had sent.
36. The 'third eye' has been described by an anthropologist as follows: *(Rai)* 'give the "inner eye" or "third eye" to the trained person. With this he can see the invisible, track an offender, and so on. With the inner eye goes the *biju*, the "aerial rope" which enables the magician to travel through the air and under the earth. Thus through submitting to "death" and receiving the inner eye, a man can receive all the occult powers with which the *rai* themselves are endowed. They themselves have the power to kill and make alive.' H H J Coate, 'The Rai and the Third Eye—North West Australian Beliefs', *Oceania*, 36:2, 1966, p.93.
37. While the country is still fairly wet after the rainy season.
38. A magnifying glass.
39. He is referring to *Mimiyagaman*.
40. 'Everybody took-em' may refer to the practice of exogamy, but the nature and fact of Paddy Roe's comment suggests that he was not referring to circumstances that could be considered normal. It is likely that it was a reference to the general post-European settlement experience of Aboriginal women of the Roebuck Plains region. As in most parts of Australia, with the growth of the European pastoral industry, Aboriginal people were dispossessed of their land and had little option but to work on European properties or move

away from their traditional lands. Western Australian Colonial Secretary's Office records, Aboriginal Department documents and Police reports show that abduction and violent coercion of Aboriginal women for labour on pearling boats and pastoral stations, and for use in prostitution, domestic service and as sexual companions was widespread. 'At two camps, the natives were lamenting the loss of their women, in each case accusing him of forcibly taking away three of their young women. I have heard from various sources that he has so committed himself for a long time past.'—A European settler's report on a pearler named Coppido, recorded in Colonial Secretary's Office report (Vol. 646. No. 153, 24/2/1869).

41. C G von Brandenstein and A P Thomas, *Taruru, Aboriginal Song and Poetry from the Pilbara* (Adelaide: Rigby, 1974).

42. Calligraphy by Chia Cheng Hsu.

43. Michel Foucault, *Discipline and Punish: the Birth of the Prison* (New York: Vintage Books, 1979), p.152, quoting J-B de la Salle, *Conduite des ecoles chretiennes,* 18th century manuscript in the Bibliotheque Nationale, Paris.

44. The only published entry under 'Roe, Paddy' in the library of the Australian Institute of Aboriginal Studies is *Gularabulu (op. cit.).* Paddy Roe's knowledge has been distributed under the names of experts: anthropologists, archaeologists, linguists and public servants.

45. Quoted in Jacques Derrida, *Of Grammatology* (Baltimore: John Hopkins University Press, 1979), p.262.

46. Edgar Allen Poe, *Selected Writings,* ed. David Galloway (Harmondsworth: Penguin, 1976), p.226.

47. Karl Reisman, 'Contrapuntal Conversations in an Antiguan Village', in *Penn —Texas Working Papers in Sociolinguistics,* 3, Austin, 1971.

48. One of the springs at *Mimiyagaman* which has a tuft of grass growing in it. (See note 55.)

49. The rainbow snake is 'lying' under the springs at *Mimiyagaman.* While the 'boss' spring has a tuft of grass representing the snake's beard, this smaller spring has 'hair' growing from his 'ear'.

50. Paddy Roe is working on a wooden lizard as he is talking.

51. I have been unable, as yet, to find out what this word means.

52. Sacred places are often approached with circumspection. The song is perhaps to let *Yungurugu* know that one is approaching.

53. 'Indit?' is a way of asking a question in Broome English, like 'Isn't it?'

54. Ray Keogh had accompanied us on this trip.

55. This is the spring called 'Nilababa' from the previous text.

56. Roland Barthes, quoted in Jonathan Culler, *Barthes* (London: Fontana Modern Masters series, 1983), p.99.

57. Ernest Jones, *Hamlet and Oedipus* (New York: W W Norton, 1949). The psychoanalytic reading tends to concentrate the meanings of the play around Hamlet as an *individual. Conjunctural* readings of texts, on the other hand, read them *in terms of what is happening at the time.* Here is Bertolt Brecht writing in Germany in about 1944: '... this is where the theatre has to speak up decisively for the interests of its own time. Let us take as an example of such exposition the old play *Hamlet.* Given the dark and bloody period in which I am writing—the criminal ruling classes, the widespread doubt in the power of reason, continually being misused—I think that I can read the story thus: It is an age of warriors. Hamlet's father, king of Denmark, slew the king of Norway in a successful war of spoliation. While the latter's son Fortinbras is arming for a fresh war the Danish king is likewise slain: by his own brother. The slain king's brothers, now themselves kings, avert war by arranging that the Norwegian troops shall cross Danish soil to launch a predatory war against Poland. But at this point the young Hamlet is summoned by his warrior father's ghost to avenge the crime committed against him After at first being reluctant to answer one bloody deed by another, and even preparing to go into exile, he meets young Fortinbras at the coast as he is marching with his troops to Poland. Overcome by this warrior-like example, he turns back and in a piece of barbaric butchery slaughters his uncle, his mother and himself, leaving Denmark to the Norwegian. These events show the young man, already somewhat stout, making the most ineffective use of the new approach to Reason which he has picked up at the University of Wittenberg. In the feudal business to which he returns it simply hampers him. Faced with irrational practices, his reason is utterly unpractical. He falls a tragic victim to the discrepancy between such reasoning and such action. This way of reading the play, which can be read in more than one way, might in my view interest our audience.' From John Willett (trans.) *Brecht on Theatre: the Development of an Aesthetic* (London: Eyre Methuen, 1964), p.201-2.

58. Paddy Roe was planning to show a collection of Aboriginal artifacts for the *Shinju Matsuri,* Broome's 'Festival of the Pearl'.

59. A kind of sandal can be made with bound strips of wattle bark.

60. Ada Janet Peggs, 'Notes on the Aborigines of Roebuck Bay, Western Australia', *Folklore,* Vol. 14: 1903. I am indebted to Kim Akerman for giving me the reference to this text.

61. I have recorded several versions of this narrative. I chose to include the most elaborate one here, recorded in 1977 at Mamabulandjin in Broome. On that occasion, people were playing cards in the vicinity, which accounts for the little girl interrupting and asking us for money.

62. In traditional Aboriginal societies where the camp is divided into two halves, incoming animals are shared equally by being split down the middle.

63. Paddy Roe had eloped with another man's wife. 'Getting clear' means facing up to the punishment.

64. Paddy Roe is called 'Lulu' in the family. The child wants money for the card players.

65. The ghost-like sound is the sound of *rai* trying to stop them from leaving the country.

66. The bark is cut from an 'elbow' in a white-gum branch or trunk to make a dish.

67. Paddy Roe's wife was confined for childbirth in a women's camp.

68. This must be Paddy Roe's wife's first husband.

69. Paddy Roe has stuck the spear in the ground and presented his thigh for a traditional punishment: spearing through the thigh.

70. Hugh Schmitt, 'Right man for the definitive book on Broome', Review of Hugh Edwards' *Port of Pearls* (Adelaide: Rigby, 1983) in the *West Australian*, 10 December 1983, p.155.

71. 'A black view of history, culture', the *Age*, 18 February 1981.

72. Henry Reynolds, *The Other Side of the Frontier* (Townsville: James Cook University, 1981).

73. This refers to Clara Jackamarra who traces her ancestry through the pioneering Roe family of Western Australia in the book written by S M Kelly, *Proud Heritage* (Perth: Artlook Books, 1980). Her exact relationship to Paddy Roe is unclear.

74. Pat Arnold, 'The Roes by any other name will always be Sandalford the *Weekend Australian Magazine*, 6-7 August 1983, p.9.

75. The holding first became known by the name 'Roebuck Plains Station' in 1918. It included a large area of land to the north of the present Roebuck Plains Station. This area later became subject of a separate lease which was taken up by George Skelton Streeter and Arthur Male.

76. Paddy Roe says that his biological father was one 'Georgie Roe'.

77. Mary Albertus Bain, *Full Fathom Five* (Perth: Artlook Books, 1982), p.228.

78. It would seem that Paddy Roe is not aware of, or concerned about, the legal distinction between owner (lessee) and manager.

79. Patrick McCaughey, *Fred Williams* (Sydney: Bay Books, 1980),

p.146.
80. McCaughey, *op. cit.,* p.54.
81. *Sunday Mail,* 25 April 1982.
82. Quoted in McCaughey, *op. cit.,* p.54.
83. Roland Barthes, *L'obvie et l'obtus* (Paris: Editions du Seuil, 1982), p.157.
84. Roland Barthes, *Mythologies* (London: Paladin, 1972), p.88.
85. Dick Hebdige, *Subculture: the meaning of style* (London: Methuen, 1979), p.104.
86. This place, Biyarrugan, is special in more than one sense. Not only does the Aboriginal oral history have it that Dampier landed here, but it is a place which is coded in the dreaming. If a spirit-god from 'the dreaming' gave humans the name of a place then it is said to be *bugarrigarra,* if not, it is just a place name, 'he nothing'.
87. The cleft stick and rubbing stick used for making fire are called *ilbi.*
88. Translation: 'Make those firesticks move Grandfather Gulbidanbidan'.
89. This is a *bugarrigarra* story which Paddy Roe tells with the help of little lizards he has carved from wood.
90. The people are travelling from south of the Fitzroy River (the Great Sandy Desert) towards Looma, now an Aboriginal community on the Fitzroy River near Camballin. There are many Nyigina people living there.
91. *Nalyag* is the blue-tongue lizard.
92. *Djaljubardju* is the name of these lizard/people.
93. Translation: *Djaljubardju ngayu*
　　　　　　　(Name) One
　　　　　　　bani wiya wiya
　　　　　　　eye small small
94. Michel Foucault, *Power/knowledge,* Colin Gorden (ed.)(New York: Pantheon, 1980) p.131.
95. Michel Foucault, *The Order of Things: An Archeology of the Human Sciences* (London: Tavistock, 1966), pp. 373-387.
96. Jacques Derrida, 'Structure, Sign and Play in the Discourse of the Human Sciences' in *Writing and Difference* (London: Routledge and Kegan Paul, 1978), p.282.
97. Percy Bysshe Shelley, *Selected Poetry and Prose,* K N Cameron (ed.) (New York: Holt, Rinehart and Winston, 1967), p.291.
98. Dampier Downs is a station in Nyigina country (see map p.59).
99. This is the 'bad' oil company.
100. Inland oil explorers clear long straight tracks through the bush to make their preliminary soundings. These are known as "cut lines".

101. This is *yungurugu,* the rainbow snake.
102. An earlier version of the fragment, along with Paddy Roe's story, 'The Good Oil Company and the Bad Oil Company' appeared in *Art and Text,* 9: 1983.
103. Grant Ngabidj, *My Country of the Pelican Dreaming* (as told to Bruce Shaw) (Canberra: AIAS, 1981) p.38.
104. Stuart Hall, 'The Narrative Construction of Reality', Interview with John O'Hara, *Southern Review,* 17: 1 March, 1984, p.7.
105. AAP and the New York Times News Service, the *Advertiser,* 2 February 1983.
106. For a pertinent analysis of sexuality see Stephen Heath, *The Sexual Fix* (London: Macmillan, 1982).
107. Derek Freeman, *Margaret Mead and Samoa: The Making and Unmaking of an Anthropological Myth* (Canberra: Australian National University Press, 1983).
108. 1 February 1983.
109. Roland Barthes, 'Languages at War in a Culture of Peace', the *Times Literary Supplement,* 8 October 1971, pp.1302-4.
110. Stephen Muecke, 'Ideology Reiterated: the Use of Aboriginal Oral Narrative', *Southern Review,* 16: 1 March 1983, pp.86-101.
111. The NAC (National Aboriginal Conference) is an elected body representing Aborigines and Torres Strait Islanders to the federal government.
112. 'Going through the law' means completing initiation rites.
113. This fragment has appeared in a more elaborate version as 'The Discourse of Nomadology: Phylums in Flux', *Art and Text,* 14: 1984.
115. Deleuze and Guattari, *op. cit.*
116. Peter Cowan, 'Broome—a Fiction', *Westerly* 3: 1983, p.77.
117. Gloria Brennan, 'The Need for Interpreting and Translating Services for Australian Aboriginals, with Special Reference to the Northern Territory—A Research Report' (Canberra: Department of Aboriginal Affairs, 1979), p.32.
118. Quoted in Henry Reynolds, *op. cit.,* p.121.
119. Geoffrey Blainey, *Triumph of the Nomads* (Melbourne: Sun Books, 1976).
120. Rhizomes, 'runner'-like structures, are used as a metaphor to combat the metaphor of tree-like structures in the introduction of Deleuze and Guattari, *op. cit.* This chapter has been translated independently by Paul Foss and Paul Patton in *I+C* No. 8: Spring 1981, pp.49-71.
121. Deleuze and Guattari, *op. cit.,* p.461.
122. Deleuze and Guattari, *op. cit.,* p.470.

123. Deleuze and Guattari, *op. cit.*, pA72.
124. Deleuze and Guattari, *op. cit.*, p.472.
125. Deleuze and Guattari, *op. cit.*, p.473.
126. Deleuze and Guattari, *op. cit.*, p.479.
127. Deleuze and Guattari, *op. cit.*, p.480.
128. Elias Canetti, *Crowds and Power* (New York: Vintage Books, 1966).
129. Blainey, *op. cit.*, pp.67-83.
130. Blainey, *op. cit.*, p.226.
131. Deleuze and Guattari, *op. cit.*, p.506.

ABORIGINAL ENGLISH

The term 'Aboriginal English' covers a range of varieties of English as it is spoken by Aboriginal people in Australia. It can vary from a mild accent to a full-blown creole language. Paddy Roe's speech lies somewhere between these two extremes, and some linguistic pointers should help the reader who is unfamiliar with the variety.

At the phonetic level, the lack of fricatives in Aboriginal languages (f, v, s, z, sh, th, etc.) affects Aboriginal English to the extent that certain fricatives tend to be replaced with stops: *this* becomes *dis, verandah* becomes *berandah,* and so on. This does not happen in every instance, variation between the two pronunciations is the normal state of affairs and it depends on a number of factors. This variation is reflected in the texts.

Extended vowels, as in *looong time,* are indicated in the text as shown. They signify duration, or distance travelled, and thus have an important narrative function. But they can also indicate hesitation, and in some cases are part of the effect of the 'growling' voice, used to indicate disapproval or disbelief.

The 'h' sound of English is not used in Aboriginal languages generally, so it tends to be 'dropped' in Aboriginal English with varying frequency. This results in forms like *'im* for *him* and other forms typical of other non-standard varieties of English.

The pronouns of Aboriginal English are special and their meanings are indicated in the glossary. Most significantly, gender is not indicated; both sexes become *he.* There is an additional pronoual 'space' in Aboriginal English, the dual. Not only are there words for singular and plural indications, but also for two people, for instance, *I, we* and *mintupella.* Different forms are used to codify whether or not the speaker includes himself or herself or the listener in the pronoun. For instance, *mintupella* excludes the listener while *yunmi* includes the listener. These forms are derivative of forms in Aboriginal languages, as is the lack of plural marking on nouns.

The semantics of Aboriginal English is also significant. Time tends to be spacialised, so that people are talked of as 'coming behind', rather than 'afterwards' or 'later'. Although Paddy Roe has learned to quantify by giving dates, times and distances numerically, it is more usual to indicate, say, quantity through an opposition between abundancy and paucity *(big mob* versus *lil' bit)*. Similarly, any position between two points is 'halfway'. (For instance when I was driving once and missed a turn-off, Paddy Roe said, 'I always miss-im myself, have to come back from halfway'.) Metaphors employed, although rare, tend to reproduce a lifestyle. A pub which has stopped business for the night might be described as 'lying down', the metaphor emerging from a culture in which the end of the day was not signalled by the closing and locking of doors.

Aboriginal words appearing in this book are mostly in the Nyigina language. The following transcription conventions have been observed: there is a three-vowel system (i, a, u); the voiced range of consonants have been chosen (b,d,dj, g, etc.) for this language which doesn't distinguish between p and b, and t and d, etc. The letter j following another consonant (1j, nj, dj) indicates that the consonant has a palatal articulation. For instance, the i in *million* is palatal and distinguishable from the i in *Bill*. R coming before another consonant indicates that this is a retroflex sound (rl, rn, rd, etc.); the tongue curves back as the sound is articulated. Double r's indicated a trill with the tip of the tongue, as in Italian. The letters n and g coming together indicate a nasal sound like the final one in *sing*, a sound which doesn't usually begin words in English. Any variations to these conventions will usually be in reference to ways of writing familiar words; the word Nyigina should thus be Njigina, strictly speaking.

Establishing the Texts

Two different conventions were used in writing down Paddy Roe's speech. The narrative style divides the text into lines, each line beginning after a pause. Pauses are indicated at the end of each line by dashes at the rate of approximately one per second. This alternation of speech and silence is an attempt to reproduce the rhythm of the narratives, and should be observed if the texts are read aloud. Narrative markers such as *so, all right,* etc. tend to divide the text into paragraphs or episodes which are also unified by changes in content, characters or movement from place to place. Gestures and other activities going on during the story are included as part of the context—the division between text and context is hard to establish even theoretically. Similarly, the role of the listener is important. The texts are essentially dialogues, even if Paddy Roe is the main speaker. His narrative style solicits audience response, and this is supported by the tendency in his culture to *collectively* produce texts. Western understandings of textual productions have tended, in the past, to emphasise the monologue emanating from a single source (the 'author'). The practice of Paddy Roe's culture fits in better with an understanding of the *dialogical* nature of language and of the text as polyphonic (an amalgam of different voices). By getting people present to contribute to the text, Paddy Roe is seeking to make his narrative relevant to the present, bringing forward voices from the past and encouraging the listener to respond to them or dialogue with them. The narrator thus attempts to repeat past experience in the present.

The other textual convention, used for interviews or talk emerging as one moves through the country, leaves spaces where there is silence and starts a new line for each new speaker. These texts are also divided into paragraphs according to shifts of content. Paddy Roe remains the main speaker since these texts reproduce his knowledges for the most part.

Glossary

This glossary includes words not adequately explained in the text, as well as words of special significance in Communication Studies and Geology:

Autochthony	(adj: *autochthonous)*—a word describing people whose life springs from their native land.
ABC	The Australian Broadcasting Commission (now Corporation).
Alluvial	(adj:) Material transported by a river and deposited, especially in flood plains.
ANU	The Australian National University, Canberra.
Balangan	Nyigina word for spirits of dead people. Butcher Joe often draws them as skeletons.
Barni	Nyigina word for goanna or iguana, a large lizard.
Big mob	A large group or amount of people, animals or things. (Ab. Eng.)
Billabong	Waterhole, pond.
Billycan, billy	A tin can with a wire handle used for boiling water for tea on camp fires.
Bloke	Colloquial expression for 'man'.
Bludger	Colloquial expression for 'lazy person'.
Boab tree	Baobab or 'bottle' tree, common in the North-West.
Bower shed	A shade structure made of a grass roof supported by four poles.

273

Brahman cattle	A modern breed of large beef cattle common in Australia's northern pastoral areas, developed from the traditional Indian breed of the same name. Most common feature is a large hump above the shoulders.
Budgerigar	A small bird in the parrot family.
Bugarrigarra	Nyigina word for 'the dreaming'. A discourse which speaks of the transcendent truths of Nyigina culture.
Bullock	Castrated bull, generic word for cattle.
Cheeky	A dangerous person or animal. Used in Aboriginal English in relation to poisonous snakes, among other things.
Chuck	Throw.
Clay pan	Dried up billabong.
Clear	To square things up, to balance whatever is owing in terms of obligation or punishment. (Ab. Eng.)
Coolamon	A traditional Aboriginal dish made out of hewn wood used mainly by women to carry foodstuffs, water or babies.
Come out in	To appear in the vicinity, to emerge from the bush. (Ab. Eng.)
Corroboree	Traditional Aboriginal dance, song or ceremony.
Country	A particular stretch of land (including waterways) unified by a number of places set out along a track or number of tracks. These places may or may not be codified in the discourse of the *bugarrigarra*. Larger or smaller stretches of country are held through complex practices of guardianship by communities and individuals. (Ab. Eng.)
Countryman	Not a blood relative but an associate connected with a particular 'country'. (Ab. Eng.)
Crook	Sick.
Damper	A bread cooked in the campfire.
Didjeridoo	Aboriginal wind instrument made from a hollowed-out tree branch.

Discourse	A term used in communication theories to indicate the modes of distribution of possible statements across lines of social difference; the elaboration of these statements into ensembles which in turn function institutionally and culturally to maintain difference; the function of *subjects* (q.v.) in relation to institutions and cultural formations and the shifting relations of power which validate knowledge and ultimately make utterance possible in specific situations. For example, the discourse of medical science imposes internal and external constraints on *what can be said* (statements) in the field. It is supported by institutions and their practices, and works continually to maintain its conditions of truth.
Down-fault	A fracture of the earth's rock layers such that a section of land slips to a lower level than the surrounding countryside.
Djila	Sacred places over which one is guardian (Nyigina).
Ethnocentrism	The largely unavoidable practice of representing others from the point of view of one's own culture.
Gardiya	White person. (Broome Eng.)
Gaze	The manner of regarding an object, the appearance an object takes in the light of specific analysis.
Goanna	Iguana, large lizard (see *Barni* q.v.)
Grog	Alcoholic drinks.
Hegemony	The processes through which a ruling minority wins consent for its practices and beliefs from the larger body of people, its maintenance of power and control over them without overt coercion.
Holiday	This term has a special significance in Aboriginal English when it refers to time 'off' white culture in order to perform necessary duties in Aboriginal culture.
Humanism/ *liberal* *humanism*	A dominant Western ideology which emphasises the 'rights of the individual', moral duties and the 'essential' humanity of all peoples.

275

Iconography	The illustration of a subject by drawings or symbols.
Ideology	Those sets of practices and beliefs, including language, which represent the world in ways conducive to the interests of certain classes of partisan groups. Ideologies work to naturalise, to make 'common-sense' of, particular practices and beliefs for those subjects who work within them.
Individualism	A predominantly Western ideology which emphasises the uniqueness of each human body and its attributes and the freedom for each person to make or break social contracts in his or her own interest. Individualism tends to underlie notions of 'free enterprise' in the economy as well as philosophical statements that the most significant meanings pertain to individual interpretations. In communication theories it tends to be displaced by the categories of 'discourse' and 'the subject' (q.v.)
Intracontinental	Occurring within a continent.
Kine	'Kind'. 'What kine?' is used as a greeting in Broome English: 'What's been happening?'
King tides	Local name for the major monthly tidal movements in Broome when sun and moon are combining their gravitational pulls.
Landsat	Colour photographic information beamed back to Earth from satellites. It is analysed by computer to reveal in different colours the mineral content of the country. It is thus very useful for mineral exploration.
Language	Used in Aboriginal English to refer to Aboriginal languages, as opposed to English. 'Lingo' is used in the same way.
Lexicon	A listing of names for things, like a dictionary.
Lil-lil	This reduplicated adjective gives the effect of 'very little'. (Ab. Eng.)
Little fella	Child of either sex. (Ab. Eng.)
Maban	Nyigina word for Aboriginal 'doctors', men and women who have attained a high degree of knowledge and

who have special perceptive and combative skills.

Magic mushrooms'   Certain varieties of mushrooms which have halluci-
nogenic properties.

Mepella   First person plural pronoun, exclusive of person spoken to. (Ab. Eng.)

Metamorphosis   A change of form by magical or natural development.

Metaphor   A figure of speech in which a word is used out of
its usual context to describe something else (eg. The
ship *ploughed* through the waves).

Mimesis   A classical term from literary studies used in this instance to describe the imitative capacity of language.

Mintupella   First person *dual* pronoun, *exclusive* of person spoken to. (Ab. Eng.)

Missus   'Wife' in Aboriginal and colloquial Australian
English.

Narga   Aboriginal loincloth.

Nicki-nicki   Plug tobacco.

Ngadjayi   Water-nymph (s) (Nyigina).

Oldfella   Aboriginal English for adult (initiated) man or
woman.

Paradox   A figure of speech which, though self-contradictory,
may present some well-founded idea.

Piccaninny   A term borrowed from American English to desig-
nate Aboriginal children.

Police boy   An Aboriginal man employed by the police as a help-
er or tracker.

Pre-Cambrian   The period of time from the consolidation of the
earth's crust to the Cambrian period, a period which
commenced about five hundred million years ago.

Proper   An adjective in Aboriginal English used also in the
sense of 'being in a direct relationship to the person
speaking'.

Reverie   A daydream or musing.

Rai	Spirits, especially spirits of yet-to-be-born children (Nyigina). Conventional spelling has been maintained. *Rayi* would be more consistent with the usage in this book.
Scrub	Bush with low-lying growth.
Sedimentary	One of the three major sorts of rock, solidified sediment of mud, sand, etc.
Shame	A category of Aboriginal English discourse evoked in relation to wrongdoing on the part of an individual, or in relation to shyness when an individual is singled out from the group.
Signifier	*Signs,* for instance words, are composed of a material element—the word as sound or trace *(signifier)* and an immaterial element, the meaning element designated by the *signified.* But the meaning of a sign cannot be empirically determined, there is no 1:1 relation between signs and the things they are supposed to refer to. Signs, and their constitutive elements (signifier/signified) are only realised in fields of *difference.* eg . We only know what 'scrub' designates through its differential relations with 'bush', 'forest' or 'grass'. Furthermore, metaphor and neologism assure that these relations remain open.
Skin	Designates the categories around which the obligations and prohibitions of Aboriginal society are organised. Most significantly, a person's 'skin' indicates whom they should marry. There are four sections or 'skins' in the Nyigina system.
Soak	A source of water usually manifested by damp ground.
Stand up	This means 'stop' in Aboriginal English hunting discourse, the moments when animals stop moving or eating and look or sniff around. *Subject* In communication theories this refers to the subjective positions individuals can take up within discourses, either in the sense that one is 'a *subject* of the Queen' (positioned in a discourse of power), or in the sense of the *reading subject of a text,* the position set up by strategies like point of view or mode of address

	through which textual meanings are realised.
Sugar bag	Wild honey. (Ab. Eng.)
Supratidal	(adj:) Above the tidal movement.
Swag	Bed-roll.
Text	Cultural artifact made up of a coded set of signs.
Think about	An intransitive verb in Aboriginal English meaning 'consider'.
Too much	A lot, many. (Ab. Eng.)
Topography	The description of the surface features of an area.
Track up	To 'read' tracks so as to find a person or animal.
Tucker	Food.
Tupella	'Those two'. Aboriginal English third person dual pronoun.
Tutelage	(adj: *tutelary)*—Guardianship, the management of an individual or population.
Utility/Ute	A car with an open back, like a small truck.
Waladja	Wild honey (Nyigina).
Walkabout	This word has a different sense for white and Aboriginal speakers. For whites it designates the 'annoying habit of Aborigines disappearing without saying goodbye'. For blacks it can be akin to 'going on *holiday* (q.v.) or as a way of *not* saying where they are going, a way of appealing to nomadism in the abstract.
Willy-willy	Dust storm caused by spiral air movement.
Yargu	Husband (Nyigina).
Yunmi	First person dual pronoun, inclusive of speaker. (Ab. Eng.)
Yutupella	Second person dual pronoun, 'you two'. (Ab. Eng.)
Youfellas	Second person plural pronoun. (Ab. Eng.)

BIOGRAPHIES

Krim Benterrak was born in Marrakech, Morocco, in 1952. His interest in painting was first formed in his own Berbere Culture. It was influenced and developed during his studies at the Ecole Superieure Des Beaux Arts in Paris from 1972 to 1976.

He came to Western Australia in 1977. He was able to establish an immediate intimacy with the local landscapes because they brought back memories of Morocco. For him, any sense or understanding of the landscape can only come from the landscape itself and such understanding can best be developed in consultation with Aborigines.

But his work is not limited to landscape, his expressionist and colourist techniques extend to other genres, like the still-life and the nude.

He has travelled extensively through many of the remote areas of Western Australia, studying and painting the landscape. In 1983 he travelled to Broome to produce artworks for *Reading the Country* and *Gularabulu*. Between 1986-1990, Krim Benterrak travelled to and lived in the Purnululu-Bungle Bungle National Park region, in order to gain a closer understanding of the landscape within this area.

Krim Benterrak's works are represented in the Australian Parliament, the Holmes a Court Collection, SGIO, Sir Charles Gardner Hospital Collection, Fremantle Council Art Collection and in private collections in France, Morocco, England, United States of America and Australia.

Krim Benterrak lives in Broome with his family.

Stephen Muecke was born in Adelaide in 1951, descendant of a radical Lutheran educationalist. He grew up in Newcastle and Melbourne, graduating from Monash University and continuing his studies in Paris, after travelling cross country from Calcutta via Nepal in the early seventies. It was in Paris that he met Krim Benterrak, when they were both students. After travelling in Europe and North Africa, and finishing his studies, he returned to Perth to work on his PhD, a semiotic analysis of oral narratives from the Kimberleys. This research involved a number of trips from Perth to the North-West, and his association with Paddy Roe began. He has taught at a number of Australian Universities, currently he is Professor of Cultural Studies at the University of Technology, Sydney.

He edited Paddy Roe's first book, *Gularabulu,* which appeared with Fremantle Arts Centre Press in 1983. *Reading the Country* followed in 1984, and *Textual Spaces: Aboriginality and Cultural Studies* (University of NSW Press) in 1992. Almost everything that he has written has had its inspiration from two things: the fact that his parents took him to Paris in 1968-9 where he was an innocent bystander in the events of May '68, and the mentorship of Paddy Roe. His writing has been enabled by a particularly supportive context: he lives in Sydney with Pru Black and their three sons, Joe, Hugo and Sebastian.

Well in Roebuck Plains Station, I s'pose sheep station, eh?
Stephen: Yeah.
Old sheep station   well where I born   I born in sheep station old sheep station used to be old sheep station   but it's finished now, but the springs is still there but them springs, they're   my *djila*   my spirit   you know   then I come out then (Laugh) baby, you know?
Krim: Mm.
But that's my spirit   an' I been, running around.

Paddy Roe was born in about 1912. He grew up on Roebuck Plains Station, near Broome in the north-west of Western Australia. He worked for many years as a drover and a windmill repairer throughout the Kimberley region. He is patriarch of a large family and has been a widower for many years.

Many of the stories appearing in this book, and his previous book, *Gularabulu*, are autobiographical, so this note is somewhat superfluous. One thing which is not stated is the importance of his life-long association with Butcher Joe (Nangan). Only in later life, after working in various capacities for Europeans, did these men take up the challenge of reproducing and promoting their own culture. According to Paddy Roe, this was Butcher Joe's initiative; the latter's paintings and pearl-shell carvings are now highly valued in Australia and overseas while Paddy Roe's stories are already being read in universities and schools across the world. In spite of his reputation as a storyteller, Paddy Roe says that his greatest pleasure is making artifacts.

CPSIA information can be obtained
at www.ICGtesting.com
Printed in the USA
LVHW100237050719
623233LV00004B/15/P